The Sound of Scripture
Reading the Bible Aloud
A brief guide for lay readers

Barbara Laughlin Adler

Lutheran University Press
Minneapolis, Minnesota

The Sound of Scripture
Reading the Bible Aloud
A brief guide for lay readers

Barbara Laughlin Adler, Ph.D.
Professor Emerita, Concordia University, Ann Arbor, Michigan

Library of Congress Cataloging-in-Publication Data
Adler, Barbara Laughlin.
  The sound of scripture : reading the Bible aloud : a brief guide for lay readers / Barbara Laughlin Adler.
    p. cm.
  Includes bibliographical references.
  ISBN 978-1-932688-78-8 (alk. paper) — ISBN 1-932688-78-1 (alk. paper)
  1. Bible—Reading. 2. Oral reading. 3. Oral interpretation. 4. Reading in public worship. 5. Lay readers. I. Title.
  BS617.A35 2012
  264'.34—dc23

Lutheran University Press, PO Box 390759, Minneapolis, MN 55439
www.lutheranupress.org
Manufactured in the United States of America

Table of Contents

Foreword

Most church-goers will immediately identify with the need for this volume as it addresses the often inferior or mediocre quality of Scripture reading in worship services. Such poor reading conveys a very negative message and is a far cry from the type described in Nehemiah 8:8 where we are told that the readers of the newly-discovered copy of God's Law "read clearly and they gave the sense so that the people understood the meaning." In the spirit of that passage, aptly quoted by the author, *The Sound of Scripture* "is designed to help make the sound of the reading agree with or complement the message."

One of the many attractive features of *The Sound of Scripture* is the use of very appropriate Scripture passages to highlight chapter themes, as well as wonderfully-fitting examples of Scripture to illustrate the type of biblical literature being discussed. Other biblical quotes provide opportunities for the reader to practice the kind of sensitive and expressive reading which the author encourages.

We applaud any attempt to improve the quality of what is surely the most important feature of a worship service: the oral reading of the Bible itself. This volume comes from an experienced and respected lay professional who is familiar with the principles of public speaking but who also clearly understands the purpose of Christian worship. Dr. Adler offers a sensitive and fresh approach which should certainly be extremely helpful for pastors, vicars, lay readers, Sunday School teachers, or any who are called upon to read the Bible in public.

Howard W. Kramer STM, Ph.D., President Emeritus, Concordia
Lutheran Theological Seminary, St. Catharines, Ontario, Canada

Introduction

They read from the book, from the Law of God, clearly,
and they gave the sense, so that the people understood the
reading (Nehemiah 8:8 ESV).

Reading Scripture aloud so that listeners understand has grown in interest among Christians of all denominations. Clergy are especially interested as are those who serve their congregations as lay readers and lectors, often the single largest volunteer group in Christian parishes. An estimated thirty-six percent of the over 313,000 congregations in the United States include lectors and lay readers in their worship services; that's close to two million volunteers—most of whom have no training in "giving the sense" with an expressive voice.

This book is intended as a guide for readers who want to become more confident and effective in communicating the meaning of God's Word clearly to listeners. Since you have this book in your hands, chances are good that you care about the "sound of Scripture" during worship services. You want to ensure that God's written words are communicated with understanding to listeners; this is a sacred and worthy goal.

So how do you accomplish that goal? While you love to read Scripture aloud, like many others you've probably never taken a course in oral interpretation and now you don't have time for it. Still, you sincerely want to improve as a reader, so that you can bring to life the rich, soul-saving message of God's words as you read them aloud.

This book will help you by first reviewing key characteristics of biblical literature and then suggesting simple methods for appropriate, expressive vocal interpretation. Clergy, lectors, lay readers, Sunday school teachers, Christian parents, and Bible study groups can learn to project the voices of ancient biblical narrators, poets, philosophers, and prophets clearly, so that "the people understand."

It is not the purpose of this book to provide a scholarly analysis of narrative literature or of any other biblical genre. It simply aims to help you discover the "essence" of biblical meaning and to express it clearly to others. Non-denominational in its approach, *The Sound of Scripture* provides a valuable resource for church workers of all vocations in every congregation. Principally written for lectors and lay readers, it will also prove useful to Sunday school teachers and parish leaders who can use it to guide others toward an understanding of biblical literature and oral interpretation.

Hidden clues for reading Scripture aloud

Not many realize it, but the Bible itself teaches us to read with faithful hearts and vocal expression. Each chapter in this book includes Bible passages (*in italics*) that offer advice for reading aloud. Several chapters provide easy practice exercises designed to strengthen your reading flexibility, as well as reflective questions aimed at helping you find the best method to use in preparing any reading.

How is the book organized?

The text is organized to guide you to: 1) understand biblical literature for its basic meaning, and 2) communicate that meaning clearly to your listeners through expressive oral delivery.

Chapter 1 provides an overview of the need for reading the Bible as literature. Chapter 2 focuses on your voice and provides practice exercises to help you develop more expression and flexibility, wjile chapter 3 describes key characteristicsin biblical literature. The remaining chapters (4-8) guide you through understanding four genres of Scripture: stories (narratives), wisdom literature (instruction), public address (prophecy), and poetry. Each genre is explained in terms of speaker identity, overall purpose or theme, and typical style of language. Finally, an appendix provides additional guidance, as well as resources for further study.

Which translation is "best" for oral reading?

Which of the many available English Bible translations should you use when preparing a reading? Some Christian denominations have adopted an official translation for use in worship, while others allow the reader to choose. Be sure you check on the preferred translation in your parish. This book occasionally uses passages from the New Revised Standard Version (NRSV), the New International Version (NIV), and the English Standard Version (ESV), all considered accurate translations. Most passages, however, are taken from the *New King James Version* (NKJV). It has the advantage of being an accurate translation and an aesthetically pleasing text in terms of sound.[1] It retains some of the poetic sound of the King James Bible, still considered by many to be the most eloquent translation.

During preparation of a reading, you'll benefit greatly if you have access to several different translations of your assigned verses. Reading several will give you a fairly strong understanding of the meaning of the passage. When tackling especially complex passages (there aren't many of those), it can help to refer to Today's English Version (TEV), published by the American Bible Society. It's a popular translation that uses contemporary language and simpler sentences in order "to make the scripture more accessible to persons who have trouble understanding the more formal translations. It has succeeded in meeting this goal, as well as offering new insights into the meaning of familiar passages."[2]

Other "paraphrase" versions (The Living Bible, The Message, and The Contemporary English Version), are easy to understand, but not as true to the original language as NKJV, NIV, or ESV. Your congregation may not want these used in liturgy due to their inconsistencies with current biblical scholarship.

Terminology

To avoid any confusion, I use the word *reader* to refer to *lectors* and *lay readers*, or any person who reads the weekly lesson(s) within the worship liturgy, or performs other parts of the liturgy, such as leading prayers, reading the Gospel lesson, making announcements prior to worship, and even delivering sermons in the absence of the minister.

Acknowledgments

I am grateful to many people for inspiring my interest in writing this book. Heartfelt, but posthumous, thanks must go to Dr. L. Lamont Okey, whose course at the University of Michigan many years ago first introduced me to the art and joy of reading Scripture aloud.

I wish I could personally thank the many students who have taken my course in Oral Reading of the Bible over the years. Their delightful energy, sharp insights, inspiring faith, and deep love for God's Word proved indispensable in identifying the key principles of good oral reading contained here. Many thanks go to several lay readers at my home congregation; I'm grateful for their heartfelt dedication to reading well, and for their suggestions in preparing this book.

With love and gratitude, I also thank my dear husband for listening to me think out loud about writing and for all the encouragement and joy he gives to me every day of our lives together.

Most especially, I thank God for the blessed Good News communicated to us daily in God's spoken and written Word. May God guide us, so that when we read from the Book, we read clearly and "give the sense," so that the people understand the meaning.

So then faith comes by hearing, and hearing by the word of God (Romans 10:17).

Chapter 1

Rediscovering
the Sound of Scripture

They read from the Book of the Law of God, making it clear and
giving the meaning, so that the people understood what was being read. . .
then all the people went away. . .to celebrate with great joy,
because they now understood the words that
had been made known to them
(Nehemiah 8:8, Today's NIV).

The Bible, like all other great literature, must be read
aloud to realize its full potential.[3]

I first fell in love with the spoken sound of Holy Scripture
while taking a course called Oral Reading of the Bible at the
University of Michigan in 1977. The instructor, L. Lamont
Okey, was a vivacious and endearing gentleman and long-
time professor of speech communication. His course was very
popular; so popular, in fact, there was a waiting list to enroll
every year. Professor Okey taught his students to understand
biblical passages as literary genre, recited in ancient times and
recorded by unique, complex personalities inspired by God.

Professor Okey taught us to faithfully read with a voice
aimed at expressing the central theme and the "personalities"
of the people, including the narrators. That class taught me a
little known secret about the Bible: Reading it aloud reveals
rich understanding and insight, and that requires diligent
practice. Although many people consider reading out loud a
routine and easy task, reading Scripture aloud is not, and
should not be, either.

When my brother, Harry, was planning his wedding, he and his fiancé, Candy, asked me to read from 1 Corinthians 13 at the ceremony. Naturally, I cherished an opportunity to read Scripture aloud, especially when it was St. Paul's beautiful "Love is patient and kind" passage. Despite my nervousness, the reading went well. At the reception afterward, a woman approached and said, very intently, "I've never heard the Bible read like that before! You sounded as if you meant it!" She sounded so surprised. Since it was a compliment, I thanked her, but simultaneously lamented the implication of her remark: She was saying that, normally, when she heard Scripture read aloud, it sounded less than meaningful, perhaps even meaningless.

Is her experience a common one? Are you surprised when you hear Scripture read with a strong voice, full of vivid and sincere meaning? Do Bible lessons sound "meaningless" when read during worship service? Meaningless readings are often delivered in a monotone voice; they sound as if the reader has no interest in what he or she is reading. The reader mumbles the words, uses a repetitive vocal inflection, volume, and rate throughout. "Meaningful" readings, on the other hand, sound as if the reader understands acutely and earnestly desires to share God's message with listeners. The reader's voice is strong in volume, and varies in tone, emphasis, and rate. Thoughts are separated logically, with pauses, making sense of each verse, and avoiding a "sing-song" delivery. Good readers sound as if they mean what they are reading!

Problems with oral Bible readings

Who has not felt dissatisfaction with the way the Bible is read in public?[4]

In the college course I teach, Oral Reading of the Bible, many of the students plan to become professional church workers: pastors, Lutheran school teachers, deaconesses, etc. On the first day of class, when I ask them to describe the sound of Scripture readings in their home parishes, I usually get a quick and strong response—sour faces, groans, and words like "awful!" "boring!" or "mediocre."

But, it's not only Christian college students who complain; ask just about anyone, and you'll get the same reaction. It's ironic that oral Bible reading has become a "forgotten art" in the Church—in the very place where the art most belongs.

Pastors and lay people agree on the reading problems they notice most often:

- mumbling
- over-articulating
- rapid rate
- very slow rate
- pausing in the wrong places
- no pausing at all
- no vocal emphasis
- too much emphasis
- monotone
- overly dramatic and "showy"
- sing-song vocal pattern

Here, I should clarify one important, and ironic, point: Although reading skills of some lectors may be weak, I have no doubt that these volunteers are devoted Christians who truly desire to share the Scripture's message with listeners. Most read the lessons with quiet reverence and respect, with earnest sincerity, and faith in the words. They are to be commended for their efforts and their desire to serve. Those who fail to communicate the powerful meaning of God's Word do so, not because they lack good intentions, but because no one ever trained them to read aloud effectively. They don't lack the *ability* to read well; they only lack the *training*.

Why is training overlooked or resisted? One important reason stems from a common misconception, heard all too often, that adults "already know how to read," after all, "we all learned how to read out loud when in elementary school." We don't need special training to do something so "elementary," right? Wrong!

Are you reading the *words* or the *meaning* of the words?

Indeed, we may have learned how to read the printed page in elementary school, but we did not learn how to read in ways that communicate the *meaning* of the passage to listeners. We learned to read and pronounce individual words; we did not learn to read the ideas, actions, moods, and images in the literature. When our elementary school teachers taught us to read out loud, they did so primarily to ensure we could recognize and pronounce words on a page. Whether we interpreted the vivid, active meaning of the words was not the goal. As a consequence, we grew up continuing to simply read words on a page, pronouncing them with little interpretation and little expression.

To better understand this dilemma, compare a lay reader with a church choir:

- They both allow active participation by lay persons in the congregation.
- They both help the worship service by proclaiming words of faith, hope, and praise.
- In both cases, their participation is key to understanding our faith.
- The congregation hopes the choir will sing well, that is, clearly, at the right pitch, and with proper rhythm. Likewise, they hope lectors will read well, that is, with clear pronunciation, strong projection, logical pauses, and meaningful inflection.
- The choir performs at its best after instruction and practice; likewise, lectors perform at their best after instruction and practice.
- The choir needs guidance and instruction by a director—someone with expertise in music and voice; in the

same way lectors need guidance and instruction from someone with expertise in reading aloud.

- Some people sing beautifully without training, but they are rare. Some may read aloud well without training. They are rare too.

Choir directors must have a variety of ways to select a soloist each week, but I'm quite sure they do not use the "grab method." They would never grab someone randomly from a pew and say, "I'd like you to sing the solo for us today." So why, when it comes to reading sacred Scripture, is this method found acceptable? Scripture lessons, delivered during traditional and modern worship services, are too important to handle casually. No parish should tolerate sloppy, unprepared readings.

Devoting ourselves to "the public reading of Scripture"

Devote yourself to the public reading of Scripture, to preaching and to teaching. Do not neglect your gift. . . . Be diligent in these matters; give yourself wholly to them, so that everyone may see your progress (1 Timothy 4:13-15, ESV).

St. Paul provides a solution to the problem. Take a look at the action words in Paul's exhortation to Timothy. He urges Timothy to apply himself to an energetic and long-term study of public reading. Paul uses several vivid verb forms to emphasize his point: "Devote yourself. . . . do not neglect. . . . be diligent. . . . give yourself wholly." Do you think he means it? And note his reason for this diligence: "so everyone may see your progress." Timothy's efforts will be long-term; he will continue to develop his skills; he will not depend solely on a quick, one-time study and then end his efforts to improve.

Whether through self-study or through an organized program, lay readers and lectors need guidance, encouragement, and an easy-to-follow process for preparing, practicing, and presenting God's Word meaningfully.

Of course, given the busy nature of everyone's daily life, that instruction must not be overly complex or time consuming. Volunteers need a simple process to follow when preparing their readings, a process that ascertains the literary meaning of the text and then "flexes their speaking muscles" so they feel comfortable reading with variety, expressiveness, and, most of all, with clear understanding.

Clear Scripture reading involves oral interpretation, *not acting*.

Reading aloud, or *interpretive reading,* is not to be confused with acting. Though both require a kind of vocal "performance" in front of a few or many people, there are significant differences between the two. The most obvious differences are visual: The lector relies on the printed page, stands relatively still, and looks at the page for much, if not all of the reading. The reader may be so familiar with the passage that sections are almost memorized, but he or she definitely holds the book prominently and looks at it throughout. In contrast, the actor memorizes the words and does not hold a script. The actor also uses props, costumes, and stage settings to portray a single character, while the interpreter merely suggests the voices of one or many distinct personalities.

Another important difference is not as obvious; it rests in the mind and intention of the reader. The actor wants the audience to believe that he/she really is the character portrayed. The Bible reader certainly does not want to "become" the voice of God or Moses; instead, the reader earnestly desires to convey to the listener the meaning and purpose of God's message for the whole community. As a reader, your attitude will greatly influence your voice and manner.

Recreating an ancient voice

> *You are a letter from Christ . . . written not with ink*
> *but with the Spirit of the living God, not on tablets of stone*
> *but on tablets of human hearts* (2 Corinthians 3:3, ESV).

Paul compares us to a letter, communicated by the Spirit of God and imparted to others—a useful metaphor for reading Scripture aloud. As we read in public, we share God's message by bringing the words to life, expressing the ideas and stories with an earnest and sincere "spirit." God's words are so much more than lines of ink on a printed page. They become alive when they are re-created as human voices in the ears of faithful Christians. What a wonderful metaphor for the lay reader: Our voices bring the message of Christ to life, and convey it to the hearts of listeners.

A similar metaphor for the oral interpretation of Scripture comes from German theologian Dietrich Bonhoeffer. Bonhoeffer was a Lutheran pastor during the Nazi regime, highly regarded for his efforts to resist Hitler's power, as well as for his brilliant essays on theology and the Christian life. In one of his works, *Living Together*, he compared reading Scripture aloud to reading a letter from a friend. Bonhoeffer suggested that when reading a friend's letter aloud to others, we naturally want to fully express the friend's purpose and meaning, but this can be done only if we understand and feel great interest in the friend's message:

> I would not read the letter as though I had written it myself. The distance between us would be clearly apparent as it was read. And yet I would also be unable to read the letter of my friend to others as if it were of no concern to me. I would read it with personal interest and regard.[5]

When interpreting Scripture we should read with "personal interest and regard," and understand the meaning of God's message to all of us. With that in mind, our vocal sincerity will express the true meaning to others.

Summary

Reading sacred literature aloud requires a great many considerations by the reader: knowledge and understanding, faith, respect, "spirit and heart," vocal skill, and physical control. Though reading individual words on the printed page might seem an easy task, *communicating* the profound meaning of the words clearly can be a complex and exciting challenge.

Perhaps the art of reading Scripture aloud is not really "lost," but only "forgotten." We can recall it if we are willing to practice and develop the art for the sake of the church. If we recapture the vitality of the Bible by approaching it as literature, our modern congregations, like Nehemiah's ancient Israelites, will listen attentively and benefit from clear understanding.

The next chapters look more closely at our preparation: How does the reader prepare and practice? What questions should you ask in understanding stories, poems, speeches, or lessons of the Bible?

Chapter 2

Creating an Expressive Voice

"Let your speech
always be gracious, seasoned with salt"
(Colossians 4:6).

Remembering the sacred source, content, and purpose of Scripture reading, those who read will want to give diligent care in how they deliver God's Word. Reading the Bible is not like reading an insurance policy; a monotone voice will not do. It is not like reading a newspaper with detached interest.

Rather, the intelligible revelation of God, who has condescended to communicate His thoughts to His world calls for reverent reading.[6]

Punctuation marks tell us where thoughts begin and end, but the human voice can convey far more meaning with a wide variety of clues—pitch variations, loud and soft volume, slow and fast articulation, stress on key words, and even pauses. Effective use of these vocal traits can do so much more for the listener's comprehension than punctuation marks on a printed page. In a way, using punctuation marks to help convey phrases and sentences is only the start of an expressive voice for oral readers.

In biblical times, without books or newspapers, the spoken word was the only way ordinary people could communicate. It was the only way news could be shared with the community. It was the only way to teach. And it was the only way most people heard and learned about God's Word.

People who could read aloud were rare; they were considered highly gifted and important to the community. St. Luke's Gospel tells us that Jesus first made himself known when he read Scripture aloud in the synagogue:

> And He came to Nazareth where He had been brought up. And as His custom was, He went into the synagogue on the Sabbath day and stood up to read. And there was delivered unto Him the book of the prophet Isaiah. And when He had opened the book, He found the place where it was written:
>
>> "The Spirit of the Lord is upon Me, because He hath anointed Me to preach the Gospel to the poor. He hath sent Me to heal the brokenhearted, to preach deliverance to the captives, and recovering of sight to the blind, to set at liberty them that are bruised, to preach the acceptable year of the Lord."
>
> And He closed the book, and He gave it again to the minister and sat down.
> And the eyes of all those who were in the synagogue were fastened on Him.
> And He began to say unto them, "This day is this Scripture fulfilled in your ears."
> And all bore Him witness and wondered at the gracious words which proceeded out of His mouth (Luke 4:16-22).

God's Word was written to be heard. Even when scribes first recorded the inspired word of God onto parchment, it was meant to be read aloud to the community; it was not meant to exist on a manuscript page, only to be studied silently in a library. It was meant to be vocalized, proclaimed for all the world to hear! And now, this is your job. You are to vocalize God's Word so that all can hear and understand.

The best way to approach reading the Word aloud is first clearly to understand the meaning of the text, and then to practice reading aloud while mentally visualizing the images, ideas, and actions. This will allow the natural expressiveness of your own voice to communicate his message sincerely and with energy.

The most common error lay readers make is to read too rapidly in a monotone voice. This chapter will help you to control your rate of reading and your tonal variety. You'll learn to speak with greater expression and modulation. However, readers must be careful not to overdo vocal modulation or read with exaggerated expression, or they risk coming across as overly dramatic, pompous, and emotional.

I like Clayton Schmidt's suggestion that the reader should "get out of the way" of the text.[7] By that, he meant that while we pay attention to reading with a strong, powerful, modulated voice, we should not let our "performance" become more "dazzling" than the message itself. Avoid over-dramatizing the passage or trying to impress the listeners. Oral reading is not acting. It's more like reading a treasured letter from a dear friend.

The LORD used to speak to Moses face to face, as a man speaks to his friend (Exodus 33:11).

Keep in mind that your goal is to read with belief in the truth, with power and sincerity, focusing on the meaning of the passage and the great news God wants you to share with all friends. Strive for sincerity as you read. Speak the words with confidence and conviction; do not exaggerate or pretend to be acting. The text should be your focus, not yourself or your performance.

I tell my students to read with their ears, not their eyes. You should hear the words of the story or poem as you speak them. Don't just look at the page and utter the words printed there. See and hear the meaning.

Your voice

What a beautiful and expressive instrument the human voice is! It can express joy, comfort, anger, sympathy, hesitation, love, fear, and a thousand other emotions. Recall how your voice sounds when you speak to a friend about some wonderful news. Your voice probably becomes rapid, with heightened energy and emphasis. Or consider how your voice sounds when you tell a friend some very sad news. You speak slowly and softly. This happens naturally, without planning, because your attitude naturally affects various modulations as you speak—loudly or softly, rapidly or slowly, and so on.

Breathing

We'll begin with the basics of breath control and pronunciation, and then review a few vocal characteristics that you can modulate when practicing and reading aloud. In general, reading out loud to a large group not only calls for greater vocal and physical energy, it requires a different kind of breathing, as well as clear, crisp pronunciation.

To practice breath control as well as clear articulation and pronunciation, try the following exercises:

1. Relax your neck and mouth by moving your shoulders up and down without moving your elbows. Now, stretch and yawn; hold the open feeling in your throat—this relaxes your throat and jaw, allowing greater flexibility.

2. Stand tall and breathe deeply from the diaphragm, then exhale slowly through the mouth. This will help you get used to an altered kind of breathing for public speaking.

3. Next, develop fuller breath control (deep lung breathing) along with smooth, clear articulation, so you can read the following poem. (See if you can get through it with one breath; no straining though!)

You're a regular wreck with a crick in your neck,
And no wonder you snore for your head's on the floor,
And you've needles and pins from your soles to your chins,
And your flesh is acreep for your left leg's asleep,
And you've a cramp in your toes and a fly on your nose,
And some fluff in your lungs and a feverish tongue,
And a thirst that's intense and a general sense,
That you haven't been sleeping in clover.

(from Gilbert & Sullivan, *Iolanthe*)

Pronunciation

If you receive no other training as a lay reader, your pastor will probably advise you to pay attention to proper pronunciation of all the words in the passage. You'll especially be concerned about unfamiliar words. I once had to read this passage from Colossians 4. It took some practice to pronounce the names smoothly. Perhaps you've been faced with challenges like this:

> *Tychicus, a beloved brother, faithful minister, and fellow servant in the Lord, will tell you all the news about me. I am sending him to you for this very purpose . . . with Onesimus, a faithful and beloved brother, who is one of you. . . . Aristarchus my fellow prisoner greets you, with Mark the cousin of Barnabas. . . Epaphras, who is one of you, a bondservant of Christ, greets you . . . those who are in Laodicea, and those in Hierapolis. Luke the beloved physician and Demas greet you. Greet the brethren who are in Laodicea, and Nymphas and the church that is in his house.*

Happily, there aren't many passages in the Bible containing so many unfamiliar names, but if you are faced with one, here are a few ways you can discover their pronunciation:

1. At BibleGateway.com, you'll find audio versions of Scripture. Listen to one or two readings of your passage and note the professional readers' pronunciation.

2. Net Ministries has a terrific website with audio files for difficult words in Scripture, alphabetized for easy searching. [http://netministries.org/Bbasics/bwords.htm]

3. Consult a Bible commentary or dictionary.

4. Ask your pastor for help with pronunciation.

However you learn to pronounce the words, be sure to practice them several times so that the sound flows "trippingly on the tongue." (You knew Shakespeare would have something to say about all this.)

At the end of this chapter, you'll find some articulation exercises—a few tongue twisters to help loosen your jaw and mouth, and help you think about articulating sounds clearly. They make good "warm-ups" for any occasion when you will speak in public.

In the next section you'll find simple, quick exercises to help "flex" your voice and body, and strengthen the various characteristics of your voice. Be sure to use these as practice exercises, but only as they feel comfortable; don't strain or overdo it. At first, you'll find that your voice sounds odd as you stretch and exercise it, which is normal. Be assured that when you read in public, you will not sound exaggerated, you will read with more expression.

Rate and duration

Rate is usually the first reading habit needing attention. Typically, beginning lectors read far too rapidly and pause between thoughts far too seldom. Some people read too slowly, pausing between every word. The average American speaks at about 200 words per minute when conversing with a friend, which is too rapid for public reading. In public, people need to *slow* the pace by almost half, to about 100 words per minute. Depending on the literature, of course, you will vary the pace between fast, moderate, slow, very slow, with many rates in between. Aim for great variety in rate, as well as variety in duration and pausing.

Rate refers to the overall speed of your reading, including the length of pauses, and the duration of time given for each word or syllable. A good way to remember to pause is to space your printed manuscript showing the pauses:

If I'm speaking quickly, my words run close together.

If // I'm speaking // s l o w l y /// my words // are // spaced farther ///// apart.

If I'm speaking // with a variety / of slow /// and fast wording, / some words / floooooow sloooowly /// andsomeveryquickly.

You can see that by spacing words on the paper with slash marks or extra spaces, you can give yourself visual cues to guide the rate and duration of your reading.

Many of my students have applied this simple technique and found it improved their readings dramatically.

Duration, or the amount of time given to each syllable, is similar to holding a note of music as we sing—for as long as four beats, or just one beat. I can utter a single syllable for a long sound, or for a sh_o_rt sound. Long duration occurs most often with vowel sounds, but consonant sounds such as S, N, M, or R, can also add length to duration. Varying the rate and duration of sounds and syllables adds a great deal of meaning to words. Think of the sound someone might make when hearing sad news, "Ooooooh"—a sound that signifies their concern or sympathy.

To get a sense of rate and duration in a text, let's consider the story of David and Goliath, where David, in his youthful enthusiasm to fight Goliath, runs toward the giant. As we read the verse, our pace should quicken to a faster rate than used while reading the action before it—after all, David is *running,* and he's a young man, so he runs *fast.*

When we read the story of Mary at the tomb of Christ, he speaks to her gently, so our voice would flow slowly with longer duration. A sympathetic or sad voice is slow, with long pauses and gentle movement, while an energetic, happy, or angry voice would speak more quickly. Think about appropriate rate and duration as you read the following passage from the book of Job. First, read it quickly out loud; then read it slowly and thoughtfully. You will hear the difference.

Naked I came from my mother's womb,
   and naked I will depart.
*The L*ORD *gave and the L*ORD *has taken away;*
   *may the name of the L*ORD *be praised.*

Pausing—"the punctuation mark of speech"

Pausing has long been viewed by speech teachers as the "punctuation mark" of speech. Sometimes the commas and periods on the page tell us where to pause, but often, pauses are needed even where no punctuation appears. Pausing should occur between thought units—wherever they are needed to help make sense of the sentence. Without realizing it, we pause during ordinary conversations quite often, and for many reasons:

- to end a thought
- to shift the topic
- to get someone's attention
- to emphasize a word or idea

Most people, when reading aloud, do not pause frequently enough, so this technique is worthy of our attention. Pauses can do more than any other vocal characteristic to clarify the meaning of a passage. You will probably need to pause between thought units far more often than you expect so use pauses liberally. The following passage from Romans 7:15-16, presents an opportunity (and challenge) for very careful pausing:

For what I am doing, I do not understand. For what I will to do, that I do not practice;

but what I hate, that I do. If, then, I do what I will not to do, I agree with the law that it is good.

Obviously, pausing in the wrong place or omitting a pause where necessary, could confuse the meaning of Paul's profound words.

Take a look at the passage below, and read it aloud in a steady stream, rapidly, without pausing:

The people walking in darkness have seen a great light; on those living in the land of the shadow of death a light has dawned (Isaiah 9:2).

Now read it again and pause when you come to a slash mark. Pause longer for two, and longer still for three slash marks:

The people / walking in darkness / have seen a great light; //
on those / living in the land of the shadow of death /// a light has dawned.

Can you hear the difference in your two readings?

Without pausing, the meaning gets lost in a steady stream of words without interpretation. A rapid, consistent rate only blurs the meaning for the listener. Your primary job as reader is to clarify the thoughts with pauses, so that your listeners hear God's message and understand it. That's why pauses are vitally important to reading any passage—complex or simple.

If the only change you make in your habit of reading aloud is to read more slowly, with logical pauses and clear pronunciation, your reading will communicate clearly.

Now read the following passages and consider the image each conjures up in your mind. What are these people doing? What are they feeling? What does God want us to understand here? After thinking about these things, determine where you need to mark for pauses as well as an appropriate overall rate (slow, fast, medium).

> *Esau became a skilled hunter, a man who loved the outdoors, but Jacob was a quiet man who stayed at home* (Genesis 25:27).

> *Esau cried out with an exceedingly great and bitter cry, and said to his father, "Bless me, even me also, my father!"* (Genesis 27:3).

> *But Martha was distracted with much serving; and she went to him and said, "Lord, do you not care that my sister has left me to serve alone? Tell her then to help me." But the Lord answered her, "Martha, Martha, you are anxious and troubled about many things; one thing is needful. Mary has chosen the good portion, which shall not be taken away from her"* (Luke 10:40-42).

Volume, projection, and stress

Volume is related to the loudness of your voice, and should be strong and confident. You might use a microphone, but that doesn't mean you can mumble and still be heard. Don't be timid! Project the words distinctly and with confidence. Of course, you never want to shout or scream—your loudness should show strength and confidence, not aggression or dominance. Along with strength, your volume should vary as you read, to create emphasis and modulation, without extremes.

Projection, closely related to loudness, refers to the distance your voice carries across a room. Projection largely depends on the strength of breath in your lungs and on your mental effort to send the sounds to the back row of listeners. In a way, you are mentally directing your voice, as if using a megaphone.

Stress is another aspect of volume, and refers to the emphasis or "punch" you give to a word or phrase. As you read and understand the passage, you'll want to stress key words with stronger volume or with pauses before and after the word.

"As action intensifies, so does the voice!"

Think of the meaning created when someone speaks with a loud voice; what about a soft voice? We are likely to speak loudly when we feel angry, joyful, or powerful. We speak softly when we feel calm or sad, loving or sympathetic. Your voice should lower or heighten in volume based on the meaning of the passage you read. The Philistine giant, Goliath's voice, as he speaks to David, might be louder than the narrator's voice. When Mary is weeping at Jesus' tomb, her voice would be softer than the narrator's.

Pitch and inflection

Just as you would not hold one note when singing a hymn, you do not want to read words in one note, in a "monotone" pitch. The *pitch* of your voice should vary up and down, between high and low, according to the meaning of the words, phrases, and ideas that you read. The related term, *inflection,* refers to the flow of your pitch. Does the passage suggest a fluid, smooth movement, or a punchy, staccato separation of each sound? The passage from 2 Kings 5 includes the voice of a frustrated, angry king, and would require a more demanding, staccato inflection, while Proverbs

31 would call for a smooth inflection, full of warmth and delight. Consider the voice of Jesus in Matthew 21, as he confronts money changers in the temple:

> *Then Jesus went into the temple of God and drove out all those who bought and sold in the temple, and overturned the tables of the money changers and the seats of those who sold doves. And He said to them, "It is written, 'My house shall be called a house of prayer,' but you have made it a 'den of thieves.'"*

He's angry, so his voice would sound hard-hitting and strong, not soft or smooth.

Compare that vocal tone to the following lines from 1 Corinthians 13:

> *Love is patient, love is kind. It does not envy, it does not boast, it is not proud. It does not dishonor others, it is not self-seeking, it is not easily angered, it keeps no record of wrongs.*

Here, we want to create a tone that is caring, fluid, warm, and soft. But even in this passage, the last clauses could become more staccato, since their meaning is not as tender as the first clauses. Don't be afraid to vary the pitch and inflection of your voice far more than you normally do. Your listeners will appreciate the clarity of meaning it creates.

Summary

The sound of your voice is key to communicating God's Scripture to your hearers; Gods' Word is meant for the ear. Your voice, facial expressions, and gestures can be dull, monotone, and meaningless, or interesting and rich with clear spiritual and emotional meanings. Richard Ward described "the public reading of scripture" as "one of those speech acts . . . that makes the presence of Christ 'come alive'" in the congregation's hearing.[8] During worship, the public reading of Scripture lessons allow God to "talk" to us directly. What a glorious gift we are given! When we read expressively, our voice becomes the tool God uses to make the sacred Word "come alive" for all who listen.

Vocal exercises

Try these for improving vocal flexibility and control:

1. Relax your jaw with a wide open mouth, and relax your lips by rounding them forward, as a "fish mouth" or a big open kiss. This helps relieve tensions in your mouth.

2. Now warm up, and relax your throat and jaw by exaggerating your jaw movements as you say the following:

- Taw-taw-taw-taw-taw-taw
- er-as-er-aw-er-as-er-aw-er-as-er-aw
- Autumn in October is often awesome and awkward.
- Pete yawns in the evening while Don tosses moss onto the lawn.

3. Feel full, smooth movement of lips, tongue, and jaw as you breathe and repeat each of the following word pairs five times. The jaw relaxes more for the first word in each pair. Use good forward mouth throughout and avoid smiling, which can create muscle tension.

- you—we
- yo'—way
- YOW—Y ——(rising pitch)

4. Exaggerate your tongue movements as you say the following:

Three thrifty rural rats ran through thirty-three thrones.
Little lambs like to loll near the large locks.

5. Exaggerate pitch and inflection

If you tend to read in a monotone voice or to mumble, when you practice, exaggerate your vocal expressiveness, mouth movements, and tonal inflections. This will not happen in front of others, but it will help you to get used to hearing your voice with clear expression.

Some final suggestions for effective vocal expressiveness:

1. Read with your ears, not with your eyes. Your voice is understood with the listeners' ears, so be sure to listen to the words as you read.

2. Don't read in a pompous tone. Avoid a self-centered focus on your own importance. You have as much to learn from the lesson as your listeners do. Be your natural, sincere self.

3. Don't read the Bible as if it were ordinary. Take it seriously and read it with humble dignity.

Chapter 3

Keys to Understanding Biblical Literature

And he has filled him with the Spirit of God,
with wisdom, with understanding, with knowledge and
with all kinds of skills (Exodus 35:31, NIV).

A poem will live or die depending on how it is read
(Billy Collins,[9] former U.S. Poet Laureate).

God's Word was written to be heard. It was written in order to be shared aloud with all of God's people. Ninety to ninety-five percent of people of the biblical world were not literate. Unable to read, they lived in an exclusively oral world. Those who could read would do so out loud, so that the entire community could hear. For this reason, the Bible is characteristically "oral" in style, focused on real people dealing with earthly as well as heavenly issues. Sentences are simple, concrete, and easy to understand on first hearing.[10]

Although the Bible speaks to us in simple, concrete words and sentences, it is both literary and rhetorical, and so communicates profound thoughts. Its dominant thoughts can be understood more readily by examining its literary style and genre. If you grasp the dominant idea contained in the specific passage, the author's identity, his audience, and the social/historical setting, you will understand what you are reading more completely, and your readings will improve noticeably.

Forms of Literature in Scripture

Most of the Bible's books can be understood according to their rhetorical or literary purpose: Does it tell a story, recite a poem, present a speech, or give advice and teaching? Theologians have categorized Scripture into multiple subcategories, including: epics, dramas, allegories, songs, prayers, epistles, legal edicts, and so on. This book groups them all into four broad genres: narratives, poetry, wisdom, and oratory. These four comprise most of the literature in the Old and New Testaments.

Narratives appear in the form of histories, biographies, or parables, such as the story of David and Goliath, or the parable of the Prodigal Son. They appear throughout the Old and New Testament.

Poetry is found primarily in the Old Testament, in the Psalms, Song of Solomon, and in parts of prophetic literature, such as Isaiah and Micah. Poetry appears only rarely in the New Testament.

Wisdom literature dominates the books of Proverbs, Ecclesiastes, Job, and a few epistles.

Oratory, or public address, dominates the prophets and the epistles, and can be found in shorter units throughout Scripture, primarily in speeches of spiritual leaders, such as Jesus, St. Paul, and the apostles.

Consider Paul's speech to the men of Athens in Acts 17 or Hosea's warnings to the nation of Israel. Oratory often appears in the context of narratives or in the form of poetry. For instance, when Paul gives a public speech in Acts 17, he does so in the context of a narrative, that is, in the history recorded in the book of Acts. The Old Testament prophets' unique oratory often appears in poetic lines.

Steps in understanding biblical meanings

Proclaiming the Word of God by reading Scripture aloud requires careful preparation. As with anything we do for God and our fellow Christians, we should begin with prayer. Pray for understanding and the blessing of God as you prepare to speak God's words clearly. Consider the following passage from Proverbs 2 as a guide:

My son, if you accept my words and store up my commands within you, turning your ear to wisdom and applying your heart to understanding—indeed, if you call out for insight and cry aloud for understanding, and if you look for it as for silver and search for it as for hidden treasure, then you will understand the fear of the LORD and find the knowledge of God.

Scripture tells us if we seek understanding and work for insight, it will come: "The Lord gives wisdom." Prayer will lead you to apply yourself to this rewarding task. After prayer, these simple steps will help you to prepare:

1. Read the passage several times to determine its central theme.

After identifying the literary genre of the passage, the next step is to understand its overall subject, its main point, and its dominant mood. Most Bibles include sub-headings for major sections of each chapter, and you can keep the sub-heading in mind as you grasp the main idea of the passage. Ideally, you should also read a few verses before and after your text. (Better yet, read the entire chapter.) What does it mean? When you've identified the dominant idea, state it in your own words so that you know its meaning. You can discover the central theme in a number of ways: from reading the passage several times, by reading three or four different English translations of the passage, or by consulting a Bible commentary. It can also help to read the other Scripture lessons of the day; they are often related in theme.

Consult a reliable aid, such as a Bible commentary, Bible dictionary, or study Bible, to discover key ideas. Ideally, every lay reader should have a good Bible commentary on hand in their library at home. You should have a basic knowledge of the historical context of the passage. Where does this passage take place? What time period? What happened previously? Who are the principal speakers? What is their identity and motivation?

2. Look for a "trilogy of meaning"

Biblical literature communicates profound spiritual meaning as well as historical patterns, and instructional guidance. Scholars have written volumes on complex interpretations. But for our purposes, simple comprehension of what I call the "trilogy of meaning" works best for vocal treatment. By "trilogy," I'm referring to texts that develop three subtexts of meanings, while also communicating one unified theme. This trilogy exists in the combined objective, emotional, and spiritual content to be found in every book of Scripture. Recognizing all three is necessary to an effective reading. We will explain the trilogy and then look at an example.

Objective messages

When reading from Scripture, we are speaking words from a world that existed 2,000 years ago, a time when social life and cultural norms were very different from ours today.[11] Understanding the culture of the Old and New Testaments allows us to understand any passage more clearly, and if we clearly understand what we are saying, we are more likely to project meaning clearly to our listeners. In Psalm 84:10, we find a simple example of how an understanding of historical and cultural meaning can clarify the meaning of any passage:

For a day in Your courts is better than a thousand. I would rather be a doorkeeper in the house of my God than dwell in the tents of wickedness.

A comparison is made here, that serving God is preferable to living with the wicked ones. But when we learn the historical meaning, that to the ancients, dwelling in "tents" would be "living the good life of a wealthy family," then the comparison becomes serving as a doorkeeper as opposed to living in luxury. Now the contrast is more striking and the picture created by these words is more vivid.

The historical meaning and theme of your passage comprise its objective (and probably spiritual) content. "Objective meaning" simply refers to the concrete subject matter of the work. What are the main ideas, concrete facts, and events? Is this a story, poem, law, or a speech? Who is speaking, and where? Can you visualize everything you are reading? Can you see the people and hear their voices as you read? You should have a clear mental picture.

It's also very important to know the meaning of each word and its pronunciation. This cannot be overemphasized. You do not have a grasp of the theme if you do not understand every single word in the passage. Be sure you know what each sentence means, and how to pronounce each word. Remember, Scripture contains almost no difficult words, so the only time you'll need to look up the meaning is when you are faced with an unfamiliar name of a place or a person.

Emotional messages

All literature, including the Bible, communicates emotional meaning. The Psalms express joy, praise, sorrow, frustration. The history of Joseph and his brothers describes a gamut of emotions—from love and jealousy to fear and courage. Biblical literature always expresses attitudes and feelings, either directly or indirectly. Look at any passage and ask yourself what moods are expressed in the passage? Do people express emotions, or is God sharing feelings? Do you find anger, love, joy, fear, or wonder?

Some passages convey a single emotion; some convey many. Consider the range of moods experienced by key people in the brief story of David and Goliath (1 Samuel 17:32-50). You'll notice that at first, Saul doubts that David can slay the giant. David fervently pleads to fight for God's people; he is enthusiastic about it! Goliath, a pompous bully, expresses ridicule and mocks David with scorn. This kind of literature is challenging because it not only communicates diverse emotions, but does so in the voices of three very different people. We will learn more about communicating the voices of diverse people in Chapter 5.

Spiritual messages

As you discover God's purpose and central theme, you will also get a sense of the spiritual message. Most Bible study guides will have something to say about the spiritual meaning of a given passage, and. of course, your pastor can assist you in determining this as well. A provocative view by many theologians suggests that all of Scripture is designed to reveal God's truth articulated in John 3:16:

> For God so loved the world that He gave His only begotten Son, that whoever believes in Him will not perish but have everlasting life.

The trilogy of meanings in "Abraham & Isaac"

Let's consider as an example the familiar story of Abraham and the sacrifice of Isaac in Genesis 22. You know the story, but you might want to read it again. As you do, visualize the people, their actions, and emotions. Consider these questions:

- What happened prior to this passage? What purpose and meaning did "sacrifice" have at the time? When Abraham is walking with his son to the mount, what is he feeling?

- Can you picture the two of them walking toward the place of sacrifice? How quickly or slowly does Abraham move? How does he feel in his heart and body, and how does his voice sound as he speaks to Isaac?

- When Abraham tells Isaac, "God will provide the lamb for sacrifice," how does his voice sound as he speaks?

- Isaac is a child; how might his voice sound distinct from his father's? What is his mood like compared to his father's? Can you picture him in your mind's eye?

- How does Abraham's mood change after the angel stops the sacrifice?

Remember, picture in your mind the people and their actions; empathize with them by imagining yourself standing next to them, experiencing the event and conversation with them. Then develop a sincere desire to vocalize God's message. Finally, as you practice and as you read to the congregation, focus your mind on the message from God, not on yourself.

Literary and rhetorical clues

Remember how your teachers always wanted you to understand every detail, every word, phrase, and sentence in a poem or story? Now you know how right they were; you must understand and visualize every name, place, description—every word—and speak them as if they were clear and concrete images, ideas, and emotions. In other words, it's important that you picture everything in your own mind and feel everything in your own heart. Here are a few techniques you can apply when you practice and read:

1. Bring out something that a casual reader might miss. Many passages that you read will already be familiar to your listeners. So, you don't want to read the passage in an ordinary way. Instead, try to discover clues in the passage that bring out deeper messages. Emphasize words that reveal the central idea. For instance, Psalm 23 is one of the most familiar passages in all of Scripture, containing a powerful image:

Yea, though I walk through the valley of the shadow of death,
I will fear no evil;
For you are with me;
Your rod and Your staff, they comfort me (Psalm 23:4).

When listening to someone read this, which words do you normally hear emphasized? You will probably say "shadow of death," "fear," and "evil," because they are vivid, striking words. But ask yourself, what is the true meaning of this Psalm? What does God want us to know? This Psalm shows us "the good shepherd"—that God is with us, caring for us, and that with God we can endure dark valleys and get through to the other side. Now, thinking of it that way, which words should you emphasize? Of course you'd emphasize "through" and "you are with me," for these words express the overall theme.

2. Take your vocal cues from descriptive clues.
In the Bible, we seldom find descriptive adjectives and adverbs. Rarely are we told what someone looks like or sounds like. So, when descriptors are provided, they must be important. They provide a cue for how we should read the verse. Look at this descriptive verse from the story of Jacob and Esau. How should Esau's words sound?

> *When Esau heard the words of his father, he cried with an exceedingly great and bitter cry, and said to his father, "Bless me—me also, O my father!"* (Genesis 27:34).

Which words gave you clues about the sound of Esau's voice? Be careful not to be overly dramatic as you read, but some subtle emotional expression must be there, even if it's only a minor change in your voice—a slower pace, longer articulation, or greater inflection. You should react subtly to the cues, not overreact.

3. Bring out words of contrast.
The Bible is rich with verbal contrast—that is, words that depict opposing images or ideas: light vs. dark, strong vs. weak, good vs. evil, happy vs. sad, and so on. It's almost a guarantee, if you look for contrast in your passage, you'll find it. Contrast is one of the most vivid and memorable uses of language. Look carefully for passages of contrasting ideas or images, and read them with contrasting vocal tones. The words reflect opposites so let them sound opposite. Here's an example:

> *Esau became a skilled hunter, a man who loved the outdoors, but Jacob was a quiet man who stayed at home* (Genesis 25:27).

As you read the description of Esau, and then later his words, how should your voice sound? In contrast, how does it sound as you read the description and voice of Jacob? Esau was an outdoorsman and hunter, suggesting a very different kind of man than Jacob, who prefers staying quietly indoors. If you react vocally to contrasting ideas and images, your reading will express the contrast and clarify the meaning of the text.

Application

Try applying these rhetorical clues to a sample passage. Choose any sequence of five to six verses and identify words of contrast and descriptive clues. What do they suggest for vocal treatment? Which words or phrases need emphasis? Where should you pause?

Summary

After praying for clear understanding and insight, consult a Bible commentary to learn about the theological and historical significance of the passage. Then, with this knowledge, imagine and picture in your mind the people, their actions and voices so vividly that you can see them and hear them—almost as if living a recreation of their experience as you read aloud.

Your ability to diligently prepare, understand, and visualize Scripture's meaning will make all the difference in the quality of your readings. Even if you choose to ignore the rest of the suggestions in this book, do not ignore the practice of mentally imagining the scene, the people, and their actions. This simple effort can help you to bring God's Word to life. You will be able to recreate God's message as the life-giving Word that your listeners want and need to hear.

Remember, the single most important step in preparing an effective reading is to understand it as a purposeful trilogy of meaning meant for the ear.

What a pleasure to hear God's messages spoken aloud so that the speaker's voice and manner convey the Bible's spiritual, objective, and emotional meanings! Since each genre is characterized by unique rhetorical purpose and literary language, the next chapters will provide specific descriptions of each.

This sharing is accomplished by a voice and body operating under a disciplined and informed mind that is cognizant of all the elements" in the literature, and "the way they operate together" to produce a totality.[12]

Chapter 4

Tell the Story:
Reading Biblical Narratives
and Histories

Jesus spoke all these things to the crowd in parables;
he did not say anything to them without using a parable.
So was fulfilled what was spoken through the prophet:
"I will open my mouth in parables, I will utter things hidden
since the creation of the world" (Matthew 13:34-35).

To read stories well, then, we need to be active—in visualizing, in imagining scenes, in entering into the spirit of events, in identifying with characters.[13]

Of four genres of literature, narrative, poetry, wisdom, and oratory, narrative makes up the majority of biblical content, over forty percent.[14] Narratives, or stories, have always been the most popular kind of literature in any culture, and biblical stories reveal to us the history and power of God. Also, we have loved these stories since childhood, and continue to love hearing them read aloud throughout our lives. Fee & Stuart correctly say that Scripture is "grander than the grandest epic, richer in plot and more significant in its characters and descriptions than any humanly composed story ever could be."[15]

Biblical narratives form a unique body of literature; the stories are not only beloved, they serve an important purpose by providing moral instruction and good news. The parables of Jesus, for instance, tell simple, earthly stories, but do so with an indirectly spiritual purpose. They often include figurastive language and symbolic images, such as "wheat and tares" or "God's right arm." The reader must find meaning beyond the concrete events in order to read the stories with understanding. Ryken explains the purpose of a parable as "a story that means what it says and something besides, and . . . that something besides is the more important of the two."[16]

Some biblical narratives, such as the parables of Christ, are very brief; others are epic in length, covering years of history about God's complex interactions with saints and sinners. Parables, epics, biographies, and histories are all forms of narrative literature. Biographies of people like Joseph, Job, or Ruth, and the epic lives of Moses and Jesus are all fascinating to hear, but even more importantly, they are inspiring; they serve God's purpose.

New Testament Narratives	Old Testament Narratives
The Gospels: Matthew, Mark, Luke, John, The Book of Acts, Revelation	The Pentateuch: Genesis, Exodus, Leviticus, Numbers, Deuteronomy, Joshua, Judges, Ruth, 1 and 2 Samuel, 1 and 2 Kings

Characteristics of narrative literature

The simplest way of understanding biblical narratives lies in finding out "what happens next" in the story: what do God and his people do and say? Who is speaking to whom? We easily grasp any story by reading it several times and looking for the journalist's five W's: Who? What? When? Where? and Why? We can also discover narrative meaning by looking for four key literary elements: narrator, setting, plot, and personalities. Understanding these, as well as their spiritual and concrete meanings, is essential to reading a narrative well.

The narrator—reader as storyteller

The first person we normally meet in a story is the narrator—that is, the storyteller. In Old Testament histories, the narrator's voice is often anonymous; in fact, scholars are not sure who wrote much of the Old Testament. Typically, it's not possible to know specifically who the storyteller is, but most narrators speak in an objective, third-person, detached voice. They report on events from a distance, usually without direct involvement in the action. As narrator, you become simply a conduit for the text. Objective narrators often seem invisible, so as reader you can adopt an objective voice. You can, as Schmit suggests, "get out of the way of the text."[17]

The authors of New Testament narratives, such as Matthew, Mark, Luke, John, and Jesus, are known to you; but you should still consult a Bible commentary in order to know them better.

The job of each narrator is to show us the scene, the people, and the sequence of events that make up the story. As reader, you are most similar to the narrator; your voice becomes the voice of the storyteller. What a marvelous assignment—that of biblical narrator! As a reader, you must identify yourself with the narrator's voice and attitude. You should approach the reading as someone who sincerely wants to share this story with others. You want to say to your hearers, "God has a wonderful story to tell us. Please listen!"

An excellent oral interpretation rests on your ability to become the narrator, whose motivation to share biblical stories remains consistent and sincere.

The setting—time and place

Biblical stories occurred in real time and space, so you, the storyteller, need to know where the scene takes place and what it looks like. Is it in the temple, someone's home, or on a mountain? Each place and setting is unique: being at home is very different from being in exile in a foreign land; talking to friends in an olive grove is very different from a conversation in a boat on a stormy sea. Knowing where and when the scene occurs allows you to visualize the setting, an essential part of a good reading.

It's equally important to sense the atmosphere of the scene. In other words, ask yourself what the mood of the scene feels like, and what happened before and after.

While some narratives give few, if any, hints as to the physical appearance of the setting, some include a very detailed description of the physical place, the weather, and the time of day. A memorable description of place occurs in the familiar opening of Genesis:

> *The earth was without form, and void; and darkness was on the face of the deep. And the Spirit of God was hovering over the face of the waters* (Genesis 1:2).

Can you picture this scene in your mind's eye? Can you imagine the atmosphere? The entire first chapter of Genesis details a description of how earth looked as God created earth and sea, day and night. By concentrating on these descriptions, imagining how it all looked and sounded, and then visualizing the serenity and grandeur of the scene in your mind's eye as you read, your voice will naturally slow down and you will appropriately communicate the awesome power and beauty of God's handiwork.

Some settings are suggested by a subtle hint. In the book of Ruth, we find a general reference to a place that might seem inconsequential because of its simplicity. But we learn later in the story that this scene is actually a pivotal event for Ruth:

> *She (Ruth) left, and went and gleaned in the field after the reapers. And she happened to come to the part of the field belonging to Boaz, who was of the family of Elimelech* (Ruth 2:3).

We learn that Boaz and Ruth's descendants will eventually include King David, so the scene depicting their first meeting is certainly significant. Also, to the ancient world, the time of year and the season were deeply felt: people were highly dependent on nature and the seasons of planting and harvest, so Boaz's invitation to glean from his harvest means Ruth and Naomi will have food for the winter.

The physical and atmospheric setting is basic to many biblical narratives. Visualizing as you read leads to a clearer reading. Not all passages describe the setting vividly, but when they do provide details, the description deserves your attention and imagination.

The plot—actions and events

Narratives almost always follow a chronological structure, and the plot follows a sequence of events. Usually, a story will build on the action and tensions will increase, leading to a conflict or a climax. As you read, notice the verbs in each verse—they are key to visualizing the actions and emotions. Biblical scholars tell us that the Hebrew people of the Old Testament viewed life primarily in terms of one's actions—what a man did brought God's immediate approval or rebuke and punishment.[18] To the Greek of the New Testament, physical actions were very important, but so were mental actions, such as thinking and questioning; pursuing philosophical understandings was the path to rightly understanding God's will.

Action verbs also provide clues to the movement or pace of your reading voice. If the scene is one of slow activity such as a conversation, you should read slowly. If the scene is one of quick movements, your voice should move more rapidly. For instance, consider the story of David and Goliath (1 Samuel 17:39-49). Look at the action verbs; you'll notice how David's movements change from slow to moderate to fast. When Saul "clothes" David in armor, David "tried to walk" toward the giant, but he couldn't, so he took off Saul's armor; then David "chooses" some stones for his weapon, and "drew near" the Philistine; finally, David "hurried and ran," and "slung" the stone.

Can you picture all of that happening in your mind? Compare those verbs to those found in the story of Christmas (Luke 2:8-9) and the moment when angels appear to the shepherds to announce the Messiah's birth:

> *Now there were in the same country shepherds living out in the fields, keeping watch over their flock by night. And behold, an angel of the Lord stood before them, and the glory of the Lord shone around them, and they were greatly afraid (Luke 2:8-9).*

Live, keep watch, stand, shine—all verbs of stillness rather than action. If you were to read the story of David with the same vocal expression as the story of the shepherds, your listeners would not hear the action, and some of the story's meaning would be lost.

Follow this basic rule regarding the flow of a narrative: Fast action = faster pace   Slow verbs = slower pace

When action intensifies, so does the voice! Likewise, when action slows down or simply describes a "state of existence," your voice should slow down as well.

Your reading should at all times convey the story as it happens. Biblical narratives are concise; they move right along without sub-plots or detours. A great deal can happen in one scene, so paying attention to the action and thinking verbs, as well as the flow of time, will greatly enhance the timing of your reading.

Another key to understanding plot is the nature of conflict that occurs in the scene. Ask yourself what kind of conflict occurs. Is it a physical battle? If so, you should picture the action in your mind as you read. Or is it an argument occurring between two people conversing? In that case, you should sense the tension within the dialogue. The conflict between David and Goliath is largely physical (although they do plenty of yelling at each other too), while the verbal tension between Jacob and Esau over Esau's birthright is purely conversational, as is often the case between quarreling brothers.

Christ's parable of the prodigal son includes a great deal of action, both physical and conversational. Read this passage and look for both kinds of action. Think about the pace you would use as you read each part of the story. What kinds of actions occur? How quickly or slowly should you read?

When he came to himself, he said, "How many of my father's hired servants have bread enough and to spare, and I perish with hunger! I will arise and go to my father, and will say to him, 'Father, I have sinned against heaven and before you, and I am no longer worthy to be called your son. Make me like one of your hired servants.'"

And he arose and came to his father. But when he was still a great way off, his father saw him and had compassion, and ran and fell on his neck and kissed him (Luke 15:17-20).

When he realizes his error in leaving his father's home, the desperate son talks to himself, repents of his actions, and plans a heartfelt apology to his father. These verses express thoughtful self-reflection—a process that feels slow and deliberate. In the next verse, as he approaches his father's home, the father runs toward him, falls on him, and kisses him—physical actions expressing great joy—a spontaneous, sudden action. This passage provides the reader with plenty of clues for thoughtful, heartfelt expression, and energetic action.

The people—personalities and voices

Now we come to the people in the narrative. In literature classes we learned to call them "characters," but I prefer to call them "people" because the women and men of biblical stories were real human beings; they were not imaginary characters. God is the central being in all biblical narratives—always present, although at times seeming to "disappear into the background" of events.[19] The earthly people are real human beings, filled with virtues and vices, like all of us. The people of biblical stories are the easiest literary personalities to understand.

Like us, the ancients loved God and their families; they struggled to live a prosperous and happy life; they laughed and cried; and they often experienced disappointment when they failed to make wise choices. Also like us, each was a unique individual. Recall some of the diverse personalities we meet in the Bible:

1. Solomon—a stately, wise, passionate, dignified, and mature man
2. Ruth—a young, devoted daughter-in-law; a humble, hard-working servant
3. Joseph—a favored, intelligent, ethical young man; an interpreter of dreams, who resists the sexual temptations of Potiphar's wife

4. David—who serves God and the people, and yet is capable of committing great sin
5. Paul—passionate preacher and teacher, who expresses great love and encouragement in Christian congregations

Each person in God's Scripture is unique, with a personality like no other. As reader, your job is to communicate the personality of each voice to your listeners. To get to know the people in the story, find descriptive information in your Bible commentary, as well as in the narrative itself. Who are these people? Ask yourself the following basic questions about their physical appearance and personality:

1. How old is each person?
2. Are they male or female?
3. What do they look like?
4. What kind of personality do they seem to have?
5. What do they do? How do they move?

Let's take an example from the Old Testament and consider a familiar biblical hero—young David, the future king of Israel.

Sample analysis—young King David

In 1 Samuel, the narrator describes young David's appearance as "ruddy, with bright eyes, and good-looking" (1 Samuel 16:12b). Besides this physical description, we can gain insight into David's identity from his actions; what he says and does tells us a good deal about him. For instance, we learn that David plays the harp beautifully and comforts Saul, who quickly comes to love David like a son. A little later we learn how brave and bold he is when he persuades Saul to let him fight Goliath, and then aggressively runs toward the giant and slays him—a young, handsome musician and giant killer! As you read aloud, visualize David and your voice will respond naturally, creating a clear image for your listeners.

David's youthful good looks, his ability to play the harp, and his energetic willingness to fight are all clues to how his voice might sound. As a youth, his voice would have been unlike

Saul's. Saul is an elderly man and not well, he is a king, and his voice would sound older, and perhaps slower than David's or the narrator's.

Motivation and mood

Another clue to understanding the various personalities in a narrative comes from your perception of their motivations and attitudes. What drives them to act? What emotions are they experiencing? King David is filled with driving ambition and desire, both when he runs to fight Goliath and when he plots Uriah's death. Jesus remains gentle and calm in the midst of a windstorm at sea, while his disciples are terribly frightened. When Jesus is in the home of Mary and Martha, Martha is "worried and troubled" about her work (Luke 10:41), while Mary calmly "sat at Jesus' feet, and heard His word" (Luke 10:39). Such contrasts are common throughout Scripture.

As you read aloud, each person's voice should subtly suggest their identity and mood. This does not mean you actually sound like the character. Instead, subtly suggest the voice as distinct from the other voices. Make only a slight change in your rate, volume, or pitch level to convey the distinctions. Saul's voice might be a bit slower in pace than David's, and the narrator's voice might be more objective or less emotional than either David's or Saul's. You could have a little fun with Goliath's voice, but be very careful about any exaggeration—keep the changes in your voice subtle and respectful. Overall, allow the dialogue between people to sound more like the narrator telling listeners what each one said, rather than like the actual "character" himself or herself.

Charlotte Lee provides this advice:

The interpreter must use his voice and body to suggest. . . . This is not to say that the interpreter of Biblical literature becomes an actor and stages a scene. But neither is he simply a reporter. Empathy, muscle tone, and posture do much to suggest strength or fear or great sorrow or joy.[20]

I want to emphasize Lee's word "suggest." Do not allow yourself to overdo different voices or body movements; that would draw the listeners' attention to you and away from God's story, where it should be. Instead, as Schmit suggested, "get out of the way" and focus on speaking sincerely, in a natural voice that only *suggests* a subtle distinction in each person's voice.

One of my favorite examples calling for subtle physical expression comes from the book of Ruth, when Boaz's kindness to her causes her to feel such gratitude, that she "fell on her face, bowed down to the ground" and thanked him sincerely (Ruth 2:10). Of course you would not actually bow, but you can *suggest* a bow by a slight lowering of your head, or allowing your shoulders to slump as a subtle suggestion of her action. You'll find that even a very slight movement or tension in your body will enhance your vocal expressiveness naturally.

Summary: Tell God's story

The single most important step in preparing your reading is to understand its literary characteristics. For biblical narratives that means having a clear grasp of your role as narrator, as well as understanding the plot, actions, place, time, and the personalities. Prepare effective oral readings by following four simple steps:

1. Read the story several times to become familiar with its plot and people.

2. Look for descriptive verbs and the actions they portray.

3. Visualize the entire scene: the physical place and atmosphere, the people and their personalities, actions, and behaviors. Do this as you practice and as you read in front of the congregation.

4. Look for places calling for short or long pauses and use them liberally, especially when actions are slow moving versus quick, or when scenes shift or people change.

5. Let your voice and body subtly suggest the voices and behaviors in the narration.

When you have a clear sense of the story and can visualize the action and the people in it, you will be able to communicate God's message more naturally and clearly to listeners. You will make it come to life!

> (Bible) stories charmed us as children, and when they are properly re-created, they hold our interest and bring us new insight as adults. Their very familiarity helps establish a sense of continuity which modern man so desperately needs. [21]

Chapter 5

Recite the Verse:
Reading Biblical Poetry

Sing to Him, sing psalms to Him;
Talk of all His wondrous works! (1 Chronicles 16:9).

Poetry is a language of images that the reader must
experience as a series of imaginary sensory situations.
The more visual we become, the better we will
function as readers of Biblical poetry.[22]

Poetry is the second most common form of literature in the
Old Testament. In the New Testament poetry is rare, but you do
find it in transcriptions from the Old Testament books, or in a
few brief sections such as John 1 or 1 Corinthians 13.

Poetry is difficult to define, but we might liken it to a
musical composition; both are meant to be heard, both express
human experience and emotion, and both please the ear with
rhythm and melody. There are as many ways of defining
poetry as there are poets, teachers, and critics. Teacher and
author Charlotte Lee defined a poem with the oral reader in
mind, as "a record of an emotional experience to be shared."[23]

Poetry is different from narrative prose because it uses
patterned language filled with images and emotions; good
poetry is dense with meaning. Narratives are dominated by
plot, action, and dialogue—characteristics generally absent
from poetry.

Although the definition of poetry seems abstract, the
language of biblical poetry is highly concrete. Psalm 8 includes words such as sheep, oxen, birds, and fish. You will

recall from English classes that the language of poetry relies on vivid imagery, metaphors, and similes. As you read a poem, the images should be vivid in your mind; visualize each picture or object. At the same time, sense the spiritual experience of the poem and the human feelings expressed, and bring the whole experience to life.

This chapter offers basic guidelines to help you discover meanings within biblical poetry. As always, you will want to consult other texts or your clergy for additional insights. The next pages will prepare you to understand biblical poetry and read more effectively along three points:

1. Emotional and spiritual meanings permeate biblical poetry.
2. Language is concrete and dense with meaning.
3. Rhythm in biblical literature occurs in phrasings, not metered rhyming.

Poetic books

Just because a passage is formatted into poetic lines does not mean its purpose is poetic. The Pentateuch and books of the prophets contain passages formatted into poetic lines, yet their purpose tends to be authoritative and historical.

In general, biblical poetry is "lyrical." A lyric poem can express a single thought or emotion, usually in very concise images. It often speaks of a specific situation with passion, expressing "the deepest and strongest feeling of the human heart."[24] With this narrow definition in mind, we can list the following books as almost entirely lyrical poetry:

Old Testament Books (primarily poetry)	*New Testament Books* (with sections of poetry)
Psalms	John
Song of Solomon	1 Corinthians 13
Lamentations	The words of Jesus
Parts of Judges, Job, and Ecclesiastes	(i.e. the Beatitudes)

Characteristics of biblical poetry

Poetry is both similar to and distinct from other forms of literature in terms of the speaker who is called the persona, its purpose, structure, and language style.

The poetic persona

Just as we identify the storyteller in prose literature as the narrator, we identify the speaker of a poem as the persona. The persona is not always known, but is usually understood to be the voice of the poet. Knowing that David wrote almost one-third of the book of Psalms can aid in imagining his identity. Other psalms were composed by unknown authors.

Most poems, psalms, and songs can speak with one of two kinds of voices: the *liturgical voice*, sometimes called the "corporate" or "national" voice, speaks as the whole nation of Israel; while the *lyrical voice* is personal, private, and speaks as an individual to self or to God in prayer.

In liturgical psalms, the persona offers a public or national prayer recited by the entire congregation, usually during worship services or special festivals. Lyrical psalms express private, personal prayers or laments and are spoken by individuals. Knowing the persona speaks with a liturgical voice should make you conscious of "proclaiming" the word as the voice of the entire community of believers. Knowing you will read a lyrical voice, means you must be conscious of reading with a private, personal tone.

Read this section of Psalm 3 to gain an overall impression of its purpose, then ask yourself if it is liturgical or lyrical:

> LORD, *how they have increased who trouble me!*
> *Many are they who rise up against me.*
> *Many are they who say of me,*
> *"There is no help for him in God."*
> *But You, O LORD, are a shield for me,*
> *My glory and the One who lifts up my head* (Psalm 3:1-3).

Next, consider Psalm 95. Does it speak with a liturgical or lyrical voice?

> *Oh come, let us sing to the LORD!*
>> *Let us shout joyfully to the Rock of our salvation.*
>> *Let us come before His presence with thanksgiving;*
>> *Let us shout joyfully to Him with psalms* (Psalm 95:1).

The first-person singular voice in Psalm 3 tells us that it is lyrical, and the first-person plural voice in Psalm 95 suggests the liturgical. Think of this distinction as the difference between your attitude and tone of voice when telling your close friend about your innermost feelings, as opposed to telling a crowd of people to "pay attention" and "listen" to an announcement.

Sometimes you'll find additional voices or speakers in a given poem. Psalm 81, for instance, provides a good example of a liturgical prayer, with mixed voices of the psalmist and God: In verses one through five the community speaks, and in the remaining eleven verses, God speaks.

Don't forget to consider the audience. Who is the persona speaking to? The listener can shift as well. If we look at Psalm 23, we might be surprised to find this beloved, familiar prayer contains a shift in audience. At verse four, the voice shifts from the objective third-person "he" (referring to God) to addressing God directly in the second-person "you":

> *He restores my soul;*
>> *He leads me in the paths of righteousness for His name's sake.*
> *Yea, though I walk through the valley of the shadow of death,*
>> *I will fear no evil;*
> *For You are with me;*
> *Your rod and Your staff, they comfort me.*

In the Old Testament, we hear the Hebrew persona, a highly emotional, passionate voice. Scholars tell us that men of ancient Israel did not withhold their feelings, instead they cried loudly and loved deeply; they let their feelings be known to everyone. Read the following lines with this in mind, and see if you find very intense, emotional language:

If I am wicked, woe to me;
Even if I am righteous, I cannot lift up my head.
I am full of disgrace;
See my misery! (Job 10:15).

This kind of strong emotion must be read with sincerity, thinking as well as sensing, but avoiding any dramatic excess. It would be a mistake to read anything in Scripture with too much emotion and drama, just as it would be a mistake to read with a dry, detached, unemotional voice. Your job as lector is to read for the true meaning—to find the balance of objective thought and spiritual truth, while remaining at least moderately sensitive to human emotion.

Historical purpose

As with any biblical literature, you must be aware of the historical setting. Although poems have universal meanings, they also have a setting— a place referred to, or an

> Don't read Hebrew poetry as if it were dry, detached, intellectual analysis. Instead, make it come alive with energy!

event that provoked or inspired the words. What was the situation that gave rise to the poem? David wrote Psalm 3 because of his escape from Absalom, which is useful information in understanding his emotional reaction. As always, your Bible commentary will be a tremendous aid in discovering the historical motive and setting for any poem.

The general purpose of the Psalms is to communicate with God, either as an individual or as a family of believers. Moreover, according to Inch & Bullock's *The Literature and Meaning of Scripture*, the most common form is the lyrical psalm. The Psalter, they write, "appears to be predominantly personal. It is a strong witness to the importance of the individual . . . (and) reveals the balance between personal and corporate identity among the ancient Hebrews."[25] Consider the nature of prayer when reading poetry in Psalms and

Lamentations. "All prayer is lyric. . . . it cannot be didactic, for we cannot teach God. Prayer is rarely dramatic, for it is personal."[26] Like prayer, many lyric poems seem to be a conversation with God.

Poetic structure

Biblical poetry may or may not follow a clear structure. Look for the introduction, body, and conclusion—the organization pattern typical of most literary genres—but don't be surprised to find a seemingly random, non-sequential series of voices, images, claims, exclamations, warnings, appeals, etc. Try reading each as a distinct thought or picture. As you do, think of the overall purpose of the piece, and approach the disconnected verses as a "list" of ideas or images within that purpose. S. S. Curry referred to this as "moving around" a central purpose: "The lyric is always rhythmic, but moves around one central theme rather than in a sequence of events."[27]

Many poems will begin and end in the same way, helping to form a circle of thought. Poems that follow a logical structure or pattern of organization will include a *fulcrum* or turning point. The fulcrum is similar to the climax in stories, and is at the key verse or emotional peak of the poem. In Jeremiah 9, the prophet's lament reaches the fulcrum at verse seven, when he turns from the sins of people to the promise of God:

5 *Everyone will deceive his neighbor,*
And will not speak the truth;
They have taught their tongue to speak lies;
They weary themselves to commit iniquity.

6 *Your dwelling place is in the midst of deceit;*
"Through deceit they refuse to know Me," says the LORD.

7 *Therefore thus says the LORD of hosts:*
"Behold, I will refine them and try them;
For how shall I deal with the daughter of My people?"

To suggest the fulcrum at verse seven, simply pause for a long moment at the end of verse six, and then read with conviction. Whether you find a change of thought, a shift in time, or a shift in voice from one person to another, take your time reading such passages. As you allow yourself to mentally shift to the new thought, so will the congregation. If you rush through ideas and voices, listeners will miss key thoughts.

In this passage from the Song of Deborah, references to time—past versus present—call for careful visualization and a reflective mood as you read:

> *In the days of Jael,*
>> *The highways were deserted,*
>> *And the travelers walked along the byways.*
> *Village life ceased, it ceased in Israel,*
>> *Until I, Deborah, arose,*
>> *Arose a mother in Israel.*

As you read the first four lines, you are reflecting on a past history, and as you read the last two lines you stand firmly in the present. Most readers overlook such shifts of structure; as lector, it's your job to bring out the meaning: "Bring out something the average, casual reader has missed." Discovering and responding to shifts in time, thought, place, or speaker is important if you are to read with understanding.

Literary language

Biblical poetry is full of figurative (literary) language. Carefully visualizing the images as you read enhances your understanding of any poem. It helps to understand any patterns in poetic phrases and lines.

Three common literary devices found in Scripture are concrete imagery, comparisons, and contrasts.

Concrete imagery

Concrete images evoke one or more of the five senses: sight, sound, touch, taste, and smell. When Psalm 57 refers to men whose tongues are "sharp swords," the image conveys that their cruel words or blasphemies wound deeply. In order to read poetry well, Leland Ryken insists that readers "think in images."[28] Look at the following from Psalm 1, and see if you can conjure a picture of it in your mind:

He shall be like a tree
Planted by the rivers of water,
That brings forth its fruit in its season,
Whose leaf also shall not wither;
And whatever he does shall prosper.

Can you visualize this person who is like a healthy tree? The last line interprets the meaning implied in the image of a tree. Concrete images can be real and imaginary at the same time; they can report actual experiences, while also conveying more complex emotional or spiritual meanings. Now, visualize each of the following; can you see the image and understand its implied meaning at the same time?

A worthless person, a wicked man,
  Walks with a perverse mouth;
    He winks with his eyes,
  He shuffles his feet,
    He points with his fingers (Proverbs 6:12-13).

I am weary with my groaning;
All night I make my bed swim;
I drench my couch with my tears. (Psalm 6:6)

The key is to see, hear, feel, taste, or smell the image in your mind, so you can convey the meaning to your listeners and paint a picture in their mind.

Comparisons

Note that the following verses are all making comparisons, utilizing metaphors and similes:

Your name like perfume poured out (Song of Songs 1:3).

The Lord is my Shepherd (Psalm 23:1).

I am poured out like water (Psalm 22:14).

His truth shall be thy shield and buckler (Psalm 91:4).

A caution regarding imagery that on first reading appears clear: Read it again (in context) for the intended or symbolic meaning. In the examples above, *"Your name like perfume poured out,"* conveys a positive thought, while *"I am poured out like water,"* intends to express the persona's weakness or sorrow. A careless reader might mistakenly read a negative image with a positive tone, or a positive image with a negative tone.

Likewise, a simile found in Hosea 13:3 appears to conjure a pleasant scene: *"They shall be as a morning cloud and as the dew that passeth early away."* However, in context, it actually expresses a condemnation of Israel. To convey its accusatory meaning, you would read the lines with a serious tone, rather than a pleasant one.

Contrast

Contrasting images and ideas create powerful messages because they tell us what something is, as well as what it is not, thus amplifying the difference between two thoughts. A well-known example of poetic contrast in Scripture is found in Ecclesiastes 3:2-8; the second verse reads: *"A time to be born and a time to die."* Two opposite thoughts or images create emphasis, and make the point more vivid and clear.

Look at 1 Corinthians 13:11:

When I was a child, I spoke as a child, I understood as a child, I thought as a child: but when I became a man, I put away childish things.

How does your voice alter as you convey the meaning of life in childhood versus life as an adult? As the image or meaning changes, let your voice change appropriately and subtly.

The "rhythm" of biblical poetry

At school, we learned to read poetry with various rhythms (remember iambic pentameter?) and sometimes with rhyming, but biblical poetry does not translate into such patterns. Instead of a poetic beat of vocal stress on alternating syllables, the lines of biblical poems follow rhythms of thought, called "parallelisms."

Parallelisms were defined and categorized by eighteenth century scholar, Robert Lowth, as "The correspondence of one Verse, or Line, with another . . . a proposition is delivered, and a second is subjoined . . . or contrasted with it."[29] The term refers to a sequence of thoughts or images which move the poem along in lines and phrases. Parallelisms are common to all oral cultures, where a thought is expressed and is either immediately repeated in different words or contrasted with an opposite thought. Lowth (and later scholars) classified parallelisms as synonymous, antithetical, synthetic, and climatic.

Synonymous parallelisms consist of two lines—the first expresses a thought, and the second line repeats the same thought, but in different words. Synonymous lines are relatively easy to spot and very common in biblical poetry. An example occurs in Psalm 51:2:

> *Wash me thoroughly from my iniquity,*
> *And cleanse me from my sin.*

The second line repeats the thought of the first:

> *wash me = cleanse me*
> *my iniquity = my sin*

Antithetical parallelisms express a thought in the first line, and then counter it with an opposite thought in the second. An example occurs in Proverbs 29:23:

> *A man's pride will bring him low,*
> *But the humble in spirit will retain honor.*

The word "pride" contrasts with "humble;" while "low" (status) contrasts with "honor."

Synthetic parallelisms express the beginning of a thought in the first line, and complete the thought in the second. In Psalm 119:140, the first line reads: "Your word is very pure." The second line completes the thought: "Therefore your servant loves it."

Climactic parallelisms are similar to synthetic, but are usually three or four lines in length. A thought begins, continues in line two, and then reaches the final point or conclusion in the third or fourth line. Here's a wonderful example from Exodus 15:10:

> *You blew with Your wind,*
> *The sea covered them;*
> *They sank like lead in the mighty waters.*

Notice how the third line makes a strong image, based on the set-up of actions ("blew," "covered") in the first two lines. In addition, the last line is longer, more final.

Here are two more examples (translated in the New King James Bible). What makes this one a synthetic parallelism?

> *The rich and the poor have this in common,*
> *The LORD is the maker of them all* (Proverbs 22:2).

What makes this one climactic?

> *I waited patiently for the LORD;*
> *And He inclined to me,*
> *And heard my cry* (Psalm 40:1).

Remember, in synthetic and climactic parallels, the thought builds to a strong conclusion, so your voice should strengthen at the end. A good principle to apply is this: "As thought or action intensifies, so does your voice!"

Summary

When preparing any poetic reading, look for all of these characteristics: persona, purpose, concrete imagery, comparisons and contrasts, and parallelisms; pull together the whole meaning as you practice. And, identifying parallel constructions can assist you in clarifying ideas, images, opposing thoughts, or climactic endings. In addition it can direct you to effective pausing between thought units. And, of course, pausing appropriately will allow your listeners to understand the sequence of thoughts, while variation in pitch, volume, and rate will communicate the human emotions so strongly portrayed in poetry.

A checklist for reading biblical poetry

1. Can you summarize the objective meaning (by visualizing the imagery and clarifying logical thought units and the "fulcrum")?

2. Can you sense the emotional meaning (with tonal color and sensitivity)?

3. Are you familiar with the meaning of its literary language (including pronunciation and meaning)? Can you visualize the images and contrasting thoughts in the poem?

4. Are you reading with a varied, sincere voice (with expressive variety in pausing, emphasis, rate, duration)?

5. Do you respond with natural, subtle gesture or physical tension (head up, subtle gesture, eye contact, subtle facial expression)?

Practice exercise

Consider the discussion in this chapter, and look at the following verse:

Thou hast beset me behind and before,
And laid thine hand upon me (Psalm 139:5, KJV).

How would you visualize and respond as you read these lines? The first line says that God surrounds the speaker with protection; the next line completes the image but personalizes it by suggesting a personal feeling of God's touch. Your voice can suggest confidence in God's presence in the first line, adding a tender, softer touch in the second. "Behind and before" portrays a sense of security, but "laid thine hand" expresses tender regard. While the objective idea of protection remains the same in both lines, the personal touch adds warmth and depth to the second.

Chapter 6

Teach Them:
Reading Wisdom Literature

> *Hear, my son, your father's instruction,*
> *and reject not your mother's teaching;*
> *for they are a fair garland for your head,*
> *and pendants for your neck (Proverbs 1:8).*

The reader must "make the listener think, and give Truth as simply and directly as possible."[30]

If we were to compare the core message of each genre we have studied so far, we would say that narratives tell stories and histories, poetry offers praise, prayer, and lamentation, and wisdom literature teaches us to think clearly and behave sensibly.

Wisdom literature is formally known as *didaché*, an ancient Greek word meaning "teachings" or "instruction." You will not be surprised to learn that a great deal of Scripture offers instruction. These writings include meditations on finding knowledge and seeking truth and instruction in understanding practical morality. They teach common sense guidance for living right—a very different message compared to sharing a story or expressing poetic thoughts.

Wisdom writings encourage listeners to live a godly life by applying sound values to everyday situations. They teach the importance of hard work, the nature of true love, the proper use of "the tongue," and even how to raise children: *"Train up a child in the way he should go, and when he is old he will not depart from it"* (Proverbs 22:6).

Advice is expressed in brief, pithy sayings, spoken aloud: *"Hear, my son and be wise,"* says a father in Proverb 23. *"My son, listen to my words, incline your ears to my sayings,"* says Proverbs 4.

Like all of Scripture, wisdom expresses profound truths in simple language. The book of Proverbs uses ordinary situations in order to teach profound lessons about living a God-pleasing life and treating each other with kindness and respect. Let's look at this genre of Scripture and identify its speakers, structural composition, and language style. Then, we will describe some vocal techniques for effective oral reading.

Books of Wisdom literature

Wisdom literature is scattered throughout Holy Scripture, in both the New and the Old Testaments. Most biblical scholars name three Old Testament books—Proverbs, Job, and Ecclesiastes—as primarily "didactic in spirit" (as Curry termed it). Most of Proverbs comprises wisdom for everyday life, while most of Ecclesiastes grapples with philosophical questions and the meaning of life.[31]

In the New Testament, wisdom writings are found in the book of James, in both of Paul's epistles to Timothy and his letter to Titus, and in all four gospels, especially the parables and other teachings of Christ. Some of Paul's writings focus on Christian theology and church policy; they include, but are not limited to, earthly matters. The gospels comprise historical narratives, but the "didactic spirit" is easy to recognize in Christ's teachings. For instance, when asked about paying taxes, Jesus says, *"Render therefore to Caesar the things that are Caesar's, and to God the things that are God's"* (Matthew 22:21). To the question, "Who is my neighbor?" Jesus tells the parable of the Good Samaritan (Luke 10:29-37), and when prideful people struggle for the best seat, Jesus tells the following parable for instruction in common courtesy:

> *When you are invited by anyone to a wedding feast, do not sit down in the best place, lest one more honorable than you be invited by him; and he who invited you and*

*him come and say to you, "Give place to this man," and
then you begin with shame to take the lowest place. But
when you are invited, go and sit down in the lowest place,
so that when he who invited you comes he may say to
you, "Friend, go up higher." Then you will have glory in
the presence of those who sit at the table with you.*

*For whoever exalts himself will be humbled, and he who
humbles himself will be exalted* (Matthew 18:8-11).

Whether spoken as a poem, story, or discussion, wisdom
literature is distinct from other forms in its purpose and spirit.

Literary characteristics of *didaché*

Now that we have a sense of the primary meaning of
wisdom literature, let's look at some of its literary characteristics.

The speaker's identity, attitude, and audience

As with other genres, you identify most with the speaker
who is speaking the words, usually a parent, a teacher, or an
elder who lovingly instructs a younger person. Theirs is a
close relationship—teacher to student, friend to friend ("My
dear brothers"), or parent to child. The speaker can be a
common person or a great king, a woman or a man (Deborah
was a judge in Israel), younger or older (Joseph was younger
than Pharoah), a father or mother, or an elderly sage. A
father offers advice to his son about seeking wisdom and
learning rather than worldly possessions or sexual excitement; Paul advises Timothy to be a conscientious leader of his
"flock;" Jesus teaches a group of persecutors how to understand justice and mercy.

The audience of each speaker tends to be one or a few
people. These are usually personal messages, filled with
warmth and sincere good will toward the listeners ("To
Timothy, a beloved son" writes Paul). Although emotional
content is minimal in *didaché*, there is deep sincerity when a
father advises his son to live a moral life, and there is Christian love when Paul urges his followers to keep order in their
congregation.

As you read these texts, keep the speaker's identity and "voice" in mind; you want your listeners to *"understand words of insight, receive instruction in wise dealing"* (Proverbs 1:2-3). You want to remember that God loves all people, and so admonishes them: *"The fear of the Lord is the beginning of knowledge"* (Proverbs 1:7). Your attitude will have a great influence on your reading. Be sure to concentrate on the deep truths in the text and then *"Raise your voice for understanding"* (Proverbs 2:3).

Structure and style

You will find wisdom literature frequently expresses thoughts in poetic forms, so don't forget to visualize and imagine the descriptive details. However, unlike poetry, its dominant message is objective or "intellectual," rather than emotional. Where poetry expresses powerful emotion, *ddidaché* does not. Nor does it speak to the entire "nation of Israel" or "the church at Rome;" it is not concerned with denominational issues. Neither is it a prayer to God. Instead, *didaché* "counsels" one or a few listeners about the practical matters of everyday life.

In wisdom literature, thought is uppermost and emotion is subtle. As we read, we offer both profound philosophical insights and sincere practical advice, focused on helping the listener understand and learn. Emotions are secondary. An example occurs in Paul's second letter to Timothy, when he instructs the young pastor on dealing with the difficulties of being Christian:

> *You therefore must endure hardship as a good soldier of Jesus Christ. No one engaged in warfare entangles himself with the affairs of this life, that he may please him who enlisted him as a soldier. And also if anyone competes in athletics, he is not crowned unless he competes according to the rules. The hardworking farmer must be first to partake of the crops* (2 Timothy 2:3-6).

You'll sometimes find unstructured passages that seem to be just a string of disconnected sayings or a list of rules. More often, as in Paul's epistles, wisdom follows a continuity of thought. Many Proverbs focus on one topic, and the structure loosely follows a logical sequence of:

- observation
- evaluation or judgment
- prediction of consequences

Consider Proverbs 1. It focuses on the topic of a quest for "wisdom." The thoughts progress in three sections: verses 1 through 7 establish the goal of attaining wisdom as supreme; verses 8 through 19 offer practical warnings about avoiding evil advisors; and verses 20 through 33 imagine future consequences of a life lived without wisdom. Notice how this passage uses figurative language (personification) to portray the abstract quality of wisdom, a very important theme in the book of Proverbs:

> Wisdom cries aloud in the street;
> in the markets she raises her voice;
> on the top of the walls she cries out;
> at the entrance of the city gates she speaks (Proverbs 1:20-21).

Proverbs 6 offers a "list" or series of brief teachings all aimed at guiding the speaker's son to making wise choices in life, such as avoiding unwise investments or business deals, the importance of hard work, and resisting adulterous relationships. You will have to concentrate as you prepare and read such passages, for while they appear simple and direct, they express profound thoughts of great value.

Jesus, in his Sermon on the Mount, offers a series of teachings, such as:

> To him who strikes you on the one cheek, offer the other also (Luke 6:29).

> Judge not, and you shall not be judged: condemn not, and you shall not be condemned: forgive, and you will be forgiven (Luke 6:37).

Scripture is full of such brief, yet profound, sayings.

Wisdom passages are a challenge to read coherently, but if you remember the purpose (to teach) and you imagine yourself as the wise teacher who occasionally rambles, your reading will sound realistic and natural.

By now, you probably have a good idea of how the wisdom speaker sounds and how to give voice to these messages. Try to communicate the profound importance of the message with a conversational, friendly, personal sincerity; your tone should sound natural, warm, thoughtful, and sometimes humorous or even enthusiastic.

One could say that didactic passages are the easiest with which to identify and to vocalize. They contain little feeling and remain sincere without becoming sentimental. Their language is simple and concise. For instance, look at this passage from Proverbs 31, describing a virtuous woman who works hard and takes care of her family:

Who can find a virtuous wife?
For her worth is far above rubies.
The heart of her husband safely trusts her;
So he will have no lack of gain.
She does him good and not evil
All the days of her life (Proverbs 31:10-13).

Familiar images like this are easy to identify; the description sounds important and sincere, not overly emotional.

As you practice reading, keep in mind that objective meaning dominates *didaché*, but don't exclude emotional meaning completely. If you repress all feeling, your voice might become monotone and the reading will sound dull.

Give careful thought to pausing, vocal emphasis, inflection, volume, rate duration, and body expression. Vocal treatment should always vary according to the thoughts and images that unfold. Contrasting phrases, profound thoughts, and visual images require your imagination, concentration, and visualization.

Application

In general, didactic passages need to be read slowly but with variation in rate. Your pitch can move in abrupt, stepping inflection, as well as smooth, sliding inflection, depending on the tenor of the thoughts and central theme. Abrupt, stepping, or "punchy" inflections will convey excitement, eagerness, or worry, while smooth, sliding inflections will convey sincere warmth, and dignified or reflective thoughts.

Let's take a brief passage and consider where we need to place pauses and emphasis. Recall our use of spacing on the manuscript (Chapter 3). Use double space lines, a large font, and dashes—or slashes / / / or spaces between words to designate pauses. Use CAPITAL letters, **bold font,** underlining, a highlighter, or any marking that works for you, to mark words and phrases that require emphasis. These markings can be used to give you clues as to where you use vocal force or duration.

Here's a familiar verse from Proverbs 11:1 (KJV):

> A _**false**_ balance (is an) **abomination** to the Lord /
> But // a _**just**_ weight // is his **delight.**

Notice the parentheses in the first line. Parentheses might suggest words that need to be subordinated or de-emphasized. Since this verse contains a warning about unfair business practices in the form of an antithetical parallelism, I would want to emphasize the contrasting words—false vs. just, and abomination vs. delight. By doing so, listeners will hear the meaning of the image and its teaching about honest business dealings.

One of the maxims for reading thought units refers to helping listeners hear the key phrases by putting emphasis on them, while de-emphasizing phrases by softening your volume: "Put the dominant thought into sunlight; put the subordinate thought into shadow." Parentheses, **bold-face,** underline, or other highlighters can give you visual clues as you read to soften or increase your volume, or quicken or slow your rate.

A caution

There are many ways to read a passage effectively. Your own voice and manner is unique, and your understanding of the objective meaning of any text will guide your interpretation. However, I want to mention one common problem to avoid when reading wisdom literature: Read instruction as a sinner, not as a Pharisee. By this, I mean you should avoid a lofty or arrogant attitude. Everything you read pertains to you as well as your listeners.

Summary

Because its purpose is instructive, your approach to reading must take on the attitude of a mentor or teacher, the one who explains real life, good values, and true knowledge. Remember that thought is dominant in wisdom literature, since it focuses on either philosophical understanding or highly practical advice.

The objective meaning and valuable insights should be clear and understandable to your listeners. Emotional meaning should be subtle; conveyed with earnest concern. As always, each image and thought should be visualized in your mind and expressed with "a deep realization of truth."[32]

Chapter 7

Proclaim and Prophesy: Reading Prophecy & Public Address

Come near, you nations, to hear;
And heed, you people!
Let the earth hear, and all that is in it,
The world and all things that come forth from it
(Isaiah 34:1).

Reading these words from Isaiah, you can almost hear the prophet's strong voice calling to all people to listen to and heed the word of God. Those who do listen and heed will have God's blessings; those who do not will have God's ultimate judgment. This verse captures the theme, mood, and sound of the fourth and final genre of biblical literature: oratory.

Oratory, also known as public address or rhetoric, includes prophetic speeches, declarations, sermons, and testimonials. It appears in poetic form and prose. Like wisdom literature, oratory's goals are instructive and persuasive. But unlike wisdom's private conversations between two or three ordinary people, biblical orators are prophets and leaders of high status who speak to large audiences—to a crowd, a city, or even a nation ("Hear, O Israel," "O Jerusalem, Jerusalem").

Oratory is unlike wisdom literature in terms of purpose and theme; it transcends ordinary life and focuses instead on God and the covenant—God's inexplicable love, saving works, and spiritual truths. Old Testament prophets speak about the future, fulfilling God's covenant, and our eternal salvation; the subject is God's divine judgment and grace, rather than our ordinary human existence.

We tackle biblical oratory after poetry, narrative. and didaché because, as Fee & Stuart said, this literary genre is "among the most difficult parts" of Scripture to understand and interpret.[1] Oratory indeed can be complex and difficult, because it includes profound prophecy, amazing visions, theological sermons, and judicial speeches—all challenging to read effectively. But now that we have studied our way through narratives, wisdom, and poetry, we are ready for the challenge!

Books of biblical oratory

Biblical oratory includes the major and minor prophets, the Pauline epistles, the book of Revelation, most of Deuteronomy, and various speeches within narrative books, such as Christ's Sermon on the Mount or Stephen's sermon in Acts 7.

There are four major and twelve minor prophets (terms that signify their length, not their importance). All prophetic books contain messages from God, sent through and spoken by fervent preachers of the Old Testament and by Jesus and his apostles of the New Testament. Through their speeches we know God's will and the future or immediate consequences promised for obedience and disobedience.

Most of the prophetic content in Scripture concerns immediate issues facing the Hebrew nation and early Christian communities. Only a few passages of the Old Testament directly prophesy about the coming Messiah. One is Isaiah's famous description of the suffering servant:

> *But He was wounded for our transgressions,*
> *He was bruised for our iniquities;*
> *The chastisement for our peace was upon Him,*
> *And by His stripes we are healed* (Isaiah 53:5).

You'll want to recognize such passages so you can visualize Christ as you interpret and read them aloud.

Prophetic writings also include what Ryken calls "visionary"[34] or "apocalyptic" literature, found in Revelation, Ezekiel, and parts of the prophets. Visionary prophecy deals with worlds beyond our own, "where ordinary rules of reality no longer prevail."[35] These texts allow us to imagine heaven and hell; they take us out of reality and into a future or symbolic world "brought about by God himself."[36] When reading visionary speeches, your ability to use your imagination and mentally visualize things you've never seen will be absolutely crucial.

Short speeches often appear within narrative texts. In Judges, for instance, the prophetess Deborah speaks to her armies before battle. In the Gospel narrative by Matthew, Jesus delivers his Sermon on the Mount. Most of Paul's epistles are essentially sermons, written to be read aloud to Christian congregations (see Romans 1:2 and 1 Corinthians 1:7). Most were not private letters to be read silently by one person; they were constructed as sermons and were written to be read aloud to the whole congregation. (Remember that most early believers could not read.)

Paul's short, evangelistic sermons are found in the narrative book of Acts. In these speeches, we hear Paul's voice speaking directly to his audience, with whom he was usually acquainted.

Literary characteristics of biblical oratory

After reading your passage for its general meaning and genre, imagine the speaker or speakers, their purpose, and their use of specific images and language. Consider this simple list of literary characteristics:

Biblical orators: prophets and preachers

How did Moses, Isaiah, or Jesus sound when they spoke? Readers can benefit by getting to know the personality as well as the persuasive purpose of a biblical orator. Becoming familiar with the speaker's personal characteristics and dominant themes will bring speakers and their messages to life, and will allow you to identify with and create a voice you can hear in your own head.

Prophets served as God's mouthpieces on earth; they preached realistically about sinful conditions and taught believers to behave righteously in order to fulfill God's plan. Berry describes the prophets as "primarily preachers,"[37] communicating orally, intent on turning men from evil. Preaching was their chief work; predicting future events was only a small part of that work.

Individual prophets of the Old Testament were similar to each other in some respects; they spoke for God with a strong, powerful voice; they reminded Israel of God's covenant, appealed to the nation's conscience, rebuked kings and priests for their sins, and expressed themselves with a righteous voice. At the same time, each man was also a unique personality with a pointed message for his specific audience. For instance, Isaiah is known as the "statesman prophet," a "prime minister of the nation,"[38] and of "noble birth."[39] His high status explains his mastery of rhetorical and literary language; some of his visions are among the most vivid and memorable in Scripture. Two familiar examples are found in Chapter 53: "All we like sheep have gone astray" (53:6), and Chapter 9:

> For unto us a Child is born,
>
> Unto us a Son is given;
>
> And the government will be upon His shoulder.
>
> And His name will be called Wonderful, Counselor,
>> Mighty God, Everlasting Father, Prince of Peace
>> (Isaiah 9:6).

Jeremiah has been called "the weeping prophet," a heartbroken man "with a heartbreaking message;"[40] he was certainly a sensitive man of deep emotions, who grieved for God's people and passionately urged them to turn from sin. Zephaniah, on the other hand, has been described as "a plain-spoken man," sober and restrained, but with impressive powers of speech in vivid and realistic language.[41] His speeches are pointed and strong. His "words concerning the Day of the Lord are among the most powerful words of judgment that the Old Testament knows"[42] Such diversity of personalities—yet all dedicated to proclaiming God's great spiritual truth!

Paul's epistles to various churches throughout the Roman world include "public sermons" (i.e., Romans, two letters to the church at Corinth, Ephesians, and others) and three letters to Timothy and Titus. Although addressed to individuals, *"To Timothy, a true son in the faith"* (1 Timothy 1:2), and largely didactic in purpose, they were certainly read aloud to each congregation. Although epistles are letters, they were all intended for the ear, written to be used as sermons and read aloud to Christian congregations.

In general, St. Paul knew his audience or had heard much about them from reports of those he trusted. Early church history suggests that Paul's letters were read with authority as well as Christian affection.

Shorter speeches, found within narrative passages, were delivered by unique individuals as well, most often by leaders or persons of high status, such as kings, queens, judges, or apostles. These orators persuaded their audiences by praising, correcting, or encouraging. With passion, they asked listeners to think seriously about civic responsibility, faith, and spiritual correctness.

The Old Testament contains a number of narrative-based orations as well, among them Nathan's rebuke of David, *"Thou art the man!"* in 2 Samuel 12, and Deborah's song in Judges 5. Deborah served as a judge in Israel, and, like a prophet, she urged her soldiers into battle with inspiring words of power and eloquence. Just imagine such orators speaking to crowds or in the courts with confidence and commitment to the Lord's work. In the New Testament, Paul's speech of self-defense before Agrippa in *Acts 26* or Stephen's fateful testimony in *Acts 7* are good examples. Both are delivered boldly, yet with deference to their contemporary authorities.

Of course, the greatest speech ever delivered has to be Christ's Sermon on the Mount in Matthew 5 and Luke 6. We all know Christ in our hearts and minds, but identifying with his voice is a daunting notion. Certainly, he was a sublime speaker. The voice of Christ, says Gundry, was "colorful and picturesque . . . figures of speech abounded."[43] Jesus used many pithy sayings, parallelisms, and even puns (although his wonderful humor doesn't always translate to English).

Most often, though not always, a prophet or preacher knew the audience personally, and, in fact, knowledge of the audience was often their motive; if people were sinning, what better reason to speak to them? We find biblical orators addressing their audiences with strong calls to pay attention: *"Hear O heavens, and give ear O earth! . . . Cease to do evil, Learn to do good"* (Isaiah 1:2, 16, 17). Or with a direct address to particular groups: *"Hear this, O priests! Take heed O house of Israel! Give ear, O house of the king!"* (Hosea 5:1). In Athens, St. Paul began with, *"Men of Athens, I perceive that in all things you are very religious"* (Acts 17:22). His brilliant rhetorical approach creates a very personal message for his audience.

Purpose and structure

As with other forms of literature, you'll want to establish in your own mind the central purpose of the message. Keep in mind that public speakers usually have a persuasive purpose and take a direct approach in confronting the audience. Biblical orators intended to bring change or gain concurrence; they preached, protested, and predicted.[44]

Prophets rebuked for wrong action or wrong belief, and they promised rewards for correct action and belief. They were very direct in their approach, in an effort to make listeners think, to awaken the nation's conscience by reminding them of God's covenant, rebuking their sin, and promising God's favor for their obedience. Contrary to a popular image of prophets, they only occasionally predicted future events with fantastic visions and apocalyptic warnings.[45]

Paul's letters, as sermons, were designed to inform, teach, persuade, encourage, and correct. Obviously, you should begin by ascertaining as clearly as you can, Paul's motivation. What has occurred to motivate this address? Find the verse that best expresses the key idea, or write out the key idea in your own words, so that you are able to focus on it as your motivation.

Public address is usually highly structured. Notice the sequence of thoughts in any sermon or prophecy: How does the speaker begin, develop, and end? An effective technique is to write out the sequence of thoughts in your own words. This will give you a solid understanding of the point-by-point development of ideas as they progress and flow.

Books of prophecy include a short introduction and then follow with the promise of doom for evil conduct, and a promise of prosperity and blessings for good conduct. Epistles and some short speeches begin with a direct address to the audience (see Philippians 1:1-3; Colossians 1:2-3), expressions of affection, a description of the situation (discord, sins, confusion, etc), and then strong appeals to Christian principles and scriptural teachings.

You'll often find Paul and the prophets using evidence and reason, while at the same time speaking with strong emotion and passion. Good examples of this structure are found in the letters to the church at Corinth and to Rome.

Although most oratory is logical in structure and easy to follow, you'll sometimes encounter sudden shifts or interruptions in the flow of thought. For instance, sometimes the prophet's voice will switch from first to third person, or from God's voice to his own (the prophet's) voice. In Jeremiah 12, we find shifts in voice between the prophet and God, as well as shifts in form, between poetry and prose.

> Righteous are You, O LORD, when I plead with You;
> Yet let me talk with You about Your judgments.
> Why does the way of the wicked prosper?

The prophet's questions are followed by God's answer (see Jeremiah 12:5-17).

Interruptions occur in Stephen's speech of self-defense (Acts 7), when the Sanhedrin stops him several times. Despite the intermittent interruptions, Stephen's thoughts follow a logical structure until he is martyred. Be sure to look for such disfluencies, so you can consciously respond with appropriate vocal treatment.

Language and style

The language of oratory creates powerful, energetic, and inspiring messages. As with the other genre, biblical oratory is rich with poetic expressions, dramatic imagery, climactic sentences, and allusions from the Old Testament. Isaiah and the other prophets often speak in poetic parallelisms, using metaphors and imagery.

> *Hear the word of the LORD,*
> *You rulers of Sodom;*
> *Give ear to the law of our God,*
> *You people of Gomorrah* (Isaiah 1:10).

Declarative sentences, rather than suggestions or speculations, abound. When Isaiah "denounces sin, the thunder of doom rolls from one sentence into the next; when he brings the comfort of the Gospel, it is as if the birds make sweet melody after the storm has passed."[146]

Dramatic dialogue between God and humans is not uncommon, calling for a slight variation of voices by the reader. Look at this "script-like" example from the prophet Jeremiah:

> *Then the word of the LORD came to me, saying:*
> > *"Before I formed you in the womb I knew you;*
> > *Before you were born I sanctified you;*
> *I ordained you a prophet to the nations."*
> > *Then said I:*
> > > *"Ah, Lord GOD! Behold, I cannot speak, for I am*
> > > *a youth."*
> > *But the LORD said to me:*
> > > *"Do not say, 'I am a youth,' For you shall go to all*
> > > *to whom I send you,*

And whatever I command you, you shall speak.
Do not be afraid of their faces, For I am with you
to deliver you," says the LORD.
Then the LORD put forth His hand and touched my
mouth, and the LORD said to me:
"Behold, I have put My words in your mouth.
See, I have this day set you over the nations and
over the kingdoms" (Jeremiah 1:4-10a).

Vocal inflection, rate, and perhaps volume must vary as the voices shift back and forth; otherwise listeners could confuse the sound of uncertain Jeremiah with the omnipotent words of the Lord!

Christ's Sermon on the Mount contains a great deal of poetic expression, beautiful metaphors such as, *"You are the salt of the earth. . . . You are the light of the world"* (Matthew 5:13-14). And St. Paul's writings are rich with poetic language as well. In his farewell message to Timothy, he combines repetitive phrasing with an athletic metaphor: *"I have fought the good fight, I have finished the race, I have kept the faith"* (2 Timothy 4:7).

Powerful language requires confident delivery and vocal flexibility. Practice oratorical readings with strong projection, dramatic inflection, appropriate pausing and volume variation. When intensity lessens, let your voice soften or lower in pitch. When intensity increases, speak more forcefully, gradually creating the emphasis that sounds natural and dignified at the same time.

Vocal treatment

The orator is confident, authoritative, so do not let yourself sound weak or timid. The orator rebukes, but does so in a loving, concerned tone, so don't let your voice sound pompous or arrogant. Look at Nathan's rebuke of King David in 2 Samuel 12. Nathan begins with a story, told to awaken David's empathy and righteous anger. At that, Nathan changes, and with passion he speaks the accusation slowly,

"You are the man," then follows with a speech of rebuke by God. The brief reproof, *"You are the man,"* should be uttered as rebuke, but with deep regret; not antagonism. God, through his messenger, Nathan, intends that David come to a consciousness of his own guilt.

Your projection should be strong, and your rate and pitch should vary expressively with the thoughts and emotions. Also, consider suggesting movements with subtle bodily expression such as gesture and posture. For instance, when Nathan speaks, his face would not be smiling, but serious; his posture would not be slumped, but upright and confident.

Contrasting images or thoughts deserve particular attention. Hosea's beautiful description of Israel restored to righteousness, nevertheless climaxes with a surprising contrasting image at the last line—don't overlook it.

> *For the ways of the LORD are right;*
> *The righteous walk in them,*
> *But transgressors stumble in them* (Hosea 14:9).

Don't let that final thought drift off with soft volume. Keep the prophetic voice clear and strong all the way. By identifying the speaker and audience, the thematic purpose, and the meaning of vivid language, you will naturally vocalize God's powerful message.

A checklist for reading biblical oratory

1. Biblical orators usually speak with confidence, correction, and compassion. A beautiful example occurs when Jesus corrects authorities with a tender image of compassion and love:

> *O Jerusalem, Jerusalem, the one who kills the prophets and stones those who are sent to her!*
> *How often I wanted to gather your children together, as a hen gathers her brood under her wings, but you were not willing!"* (Luke 13:34).

2. Direct your voice to the back row. Strong projection is key for oratory. In general, keep volume strong, but varied.

3. Sincerity is largely conveyed by mild inflectional "gliding" in the voice. But, emphatic reason and careful thinking may call for a stepping inflection. Does the speaker rebuke the audience? Or express concern and love? Or both?

4. Look for key words and strong commands. Where must you create emphasis? Which words call for vocal stress or force?

5. Be sure to vary the rate from moderate to slow. Prophecy and oratory are seldom delivered with rapid rate and duration. Take your time. Where must you pause?

6. What is the tonal color of this passage? What emotions dominate? While prophets are seen as stern judges, your voice should not give way to harsh denunciation, but must aim for making listeners think and feel for themselves; Curry taught that "righteous indignation must never degenerate into anger. The prophet continually shows love for his country and profound regret at the sins of his people."[47]

Summary

The wonderful beauty and passion of Hebrew oratory and Greek evangelism deserve faithful sincerity and affectionate dignity by the reader. As you discover the unique personality of individual speakers and the trilogy of meaning in their messages, you will come to identify with the urgent necessity of proclaiming God's Holy Word. What a joy to know that your voice can help communicate its life-giving hope!

> "Shout it aloud, do not hold back. Raise your voice like a trumpet. Declare to my people their rebellion"
> (Isaiah 58:1, NIV).

Appendix A

Top Eleven Techniques for Reading Scripture Aloud

There is no "one best way" to read Scripture aloud. Your reading should reflect your understanding of the thoughts, themes, images, and emotions of the work. However, there are some general guidelines or principles for approaching literature and interpreting a biblical text which should help you to stay true to its "trilogy of meaning, and to get out of the way of the text."

1. "Devote yourself to the public reading of Scripture."

Don't let anyone look down on you because you are young, but set an example for the believers in speech, in conduct, in love, in faith and in purity. Until I come, devote yourself to the public reading of Scripture. . . (1 Timothy 4:12-13a, NIV, 2011).

2. Prepare every reading with devotion and diligence.

Study the passage for its trilogy of meaning, its Holy purpose and genre, its narrator/persona/speaker, historical setting, structure, and its literary language. When practicing, exaggerate your vocal expressiveness. This will "train" you to feel accustomed to reading the passage aloud in public, with clear interpretation.

3. Read with your ears, not with your eyes.

Concentrate and listen to the meaning as you read. "Hear" the lesson, see the images and actions,don't just read the words on the page.

4. Read the meaning, not the words.

Shake off a routine or mechanical approach to reading. Instead, visualize the details in your mind, bring the meaning of the image, thought, and action to life! Let meaning sound clearly

5. Bring out something in your reading that the average reader might have missed.

> . . . *though I walk through the valley of the shadow of death, I will fear no evil. . ."* (Psalm 23:4).

"Shadow of death" calls to mind a vivid image, but it is not the point of the verse or the poem. The key message of Psalm 23 is that the shepherd will watch over us and care for us; he will take us from death to life. Emphasis should fall on the word "through" since we will pass through troubles on our way to his kingdom. Sometimes the obviously vivid words are not the keys to the message contained in the passage. Place vocal emphasis on key words and phrases discovered in your preparation.

6. Watch for verbal signposts: "Behold," "Lo," "Thus says the Lord"

Pause before and/or after important words. This will draw attention to the statement following.

7. Take your cue from a clue.

> *Esau cried out with an exceedingly great and bitter cry, and said to his father, "Bless me, even me also, my father!" (Genesis 27:34).*

Adjectives and adverbs are rare in Scripture, so when you find them, they are significant—that is, they have something to do with clear visualization and understanding of the passage.

8. Watch for words of contrast.

> *Esau became a skilled hunter, a man who loved the outdoors, but Jacob was a quiet man who stayed at home* (Genesis 25:27).

Your voice can subtly suggest the contrast of images or ideas. One might be negative, the other positive. One might describe sin, the other righteousness. One might show anger, the other love, and so on. Your tone of voice should reflect the meaning of contrasting thoughts.

9. Don't read with a haughty tone of voice.

Read with sincerity. You are just as much a sinner as your audience, so do not read with a haughty, "holier-than-thou" attitude. Instead, read sincerely. Sincerity in your voice is essential. In your own mind, understand what you read, and concentrate on the objective, emotional, and spiritual meanings of the passages.

10. Do not read the Bible as if it were ordinary.

You must not read Scripture in the same way that you read a newspaper article aloud. Read the Bible with sincere respect, with confidence in its truth and a joyful desire to share it with the congregation.

11. Do not read Law as if it were Gospel or Gospel as if it were Law.

God's Word contains judgments and grace. Be sure you vocally distinguish the meaning of Law passages with a subtle tone of "judgment," and Gospel passages with a subtle tone of loving "grace." Both messages appear in both testaments.

Appendix B

The Bible's Mandate: Read it Aloud!

If we let Scripture speak for itself, it will tell us, in every literary form—poetry, narrative, didaché, and oratory—to share God's Word out loud!

When you get to Babylon, see that you read all these words aloud (Jeremiah 51:61, NIV).

Blessed is the one who reads aloud the words of this prophecy, and blessed are those who hear it and take to heart what is written in it (Revelation 1:3, NIV).

Shout it aloud, do not hold back. Raise your voice like a trumpet (Isaiah 58:1, NIV).

Sing, O daughter of Zion! Shout, O Israel! Be glad and rejoice with all your heart, O daughter of Jerusalem! (Zephaniah 3:14, NKJV).

He read it aloud from daybreak till noon as he faced the square before the Water Gate in the presence of the men, women and others who could understand. And all the people listened attentively to the Book of the Law (Nehemiah 8:3, NIV).

Proclaiming aloud your praise and telling of all your wonderful deeds (Psalm 26:7, NIV).

My son, if you receive my words, And treasure my commands within you, So that you incline your ear to wisdom, And apply your heart to understanding;

Yes, if you cry out for discernment, And lift up your voice for understanding, If you seek her as silver, And search for her as for hidden treasures; Then you will understand the fear of the LORD, And find the knowledge of God. For the LORD gives wisdom; From His mouth come knowledge and understanding (Proverbs 2:1-6, NKJV).

Unless you speak intelligible words with your tongue, how will anyone know what you are saying? You will just be speaking into the air (1Corinthians 14:9, NIV)..

So then faith comes by hearing, and hearing by the word of God (Romans 10:17, NKJV).

Final words from a poet and a teacher

Bring the whole soul of man into activity...I feel strongly and I think strongly, but I seldom feel without thinking or think without feeling (Samuel Taylor Coleridge).

Vivid and emotionally toned action material will hold attention; abstract philosophical thought will not....The ear prefers simplicity to complexity, concreteness to generality, and vivid imagery to vague abstraction (Louise Scrivner).

Bibliography

Adler, Barbara Laughlin. "Congregational Lay Reader Programs," unpublished survey of 500 Lutheran, Presbyterian, Episcopalian, Baptist, Methodist clergy and church workers in Michigan, 2007.

Alter, Robert. *The Art of Biblical Narrative* (New York: Basic Books, 1981).

Berry, George Ricker. "The apocalyptic literature of the Old Testament," *Journal of Biblical Literature 62*, no. 1 (January 1, 1943): 9-16.

Bilezikian, Gilbert G. "Interpreting Apocalyptic Literature," in *The Literature and Meaning of Scripture*, Morris A. Inch and C. Hassell Bullock, eds. (Grand Rapids, Michigan: Baker Book House, 1981).

Bonhoeffer, Dietrich. *Life Together* (New York: Harper & Row, 1954).

Brooks, Keith, Eugene Bahn, and L. Lamont Okey. *The Communicative Act of Oral Interpretation* (Boston: Allyn & Bacon, 1975).

Curry, Samuel Silas. *Vocal and Literary Interpretation of the Bible* (New York: MacMillan, 1903).

Eliot, Thomas Stearns. "The Use of Poetry and The Use of Criticism," in *Selected Prose of T. S. Eliot*, Frank Kermode, ed. (Orlando, Florida: Houghton Mifflin Harcourt, 1975): 79-96.

Fee, Gordon and Douglas Stuart. *How to Read the Bible for All its Worth*, 2nd Ed. (Grand Rapids, Michigan: Zondervan, 1993).

Felton, Gayle Carlton. "Which Translation is Best?" *The Upper Room*, August 2007, accessed 6 July 2011. http://www.upperroom.org/reflections/default.asp? act=display_content&itemid=180268.

Fitzgerald, Jon M. *Speech Activities of the Michigan Interscholastic Forensics Association* (Ann Arbor, Michigan: University of Michigan, 1983).

Gamble, Harry Y. *Books and Readers in the Early Church: A History of Early Christian Texts* (New Haven, Connecticut: Yale University Press, 1995).

Gottlieb, Marvin R. *Oral Interpretation* (New York: McGraw-Hill, 1980).

Gundry, Robert H. 1970. *A Survey of the New Testament* (Grand Rapids, Michigan: Zondervan).

Harwell, Charles W. and Daniel McDonald, eds. *The Bible: A Literary Survey* (Indianapolis: Bobbs-Merrill, 1975).

Inch, Morris A. *The Literature and Meaning of Scripture*. Morris A. Inch and C. Hassell Bullock, eds. (Grand Rapids, Michigan: Baker Book House, 1981).

Juel, Donald, "The Strange Silence of the Bible," *Interpretation 51*, (1997): 5-19.

Kent, Grenville J. R, Paul J. Kissling, and Laurence A. Turner, eds. *Reclaiming the Old Testament for Christian Preaching* (Downers Grove, Illinois: IVP Academic, 2010).

Lee, Charlotte I. *Oral Reading of the Scriptures* (New York: Houghton, Mifflin, Harcourt, 1974).

Lewis, C. S. *Reflections on the Psalms* (San Diego: Harcourt, 1986).

Lowth, Robert. *Lectures on the Sacred Poetry of the Hebrews,* G. Gregory, tr., 1839, in *Landmarks of World Literature: The Bible* by Stephen Prickett and Robert Barnes (Cambridge, England: Cambridge University Press, 1991).

McWilliams, Barry. "Discerning the Story Structures in the Narrative Literature of the Bible." *The Art of Telling Stories.* 2002, accessed 25 March 2011, http://www.eldrbarry.net/mous/bibl/narr.htm.

Ortlieb, Evan, Neva Cramer, and Earl Cheek, Jr. "The art of reading: dramatizing literacy," *Reading Improvement* (Fall 2007), accessed 7 June 2011. http://findarticles.com/p/articles/mi_hb6516/is_3_44/ai_n29383542/tag=mantle_skin;content.

Powell, Mark Allan. "Law and Gospel Bring God's Word: Listen for Each As You Hear the Sunday Lessons," *The Lutheran* (February 2009), http://www.thelutheran.org/article/article.cfm?article_id=7728&key=5972198.

Roehrs, Walter R. and Martin H. Franzmann. *Concordia Self-Study Commentary* (St. Louis: Concordia Publishing House, 1979).

Ryken, Leland. *How to Read the Bible as Literature . . . and Get More Out of It* (Grand Rapids, Michigan: Zondervan, 1984).

Schmit, Clayton J. *Public Reading of Scripture: A Handbook* (Nashville, Tennessee: Abingdon Press, 2002).

Scrivner, Louise and Dan Robinette. *A Guide to Oral Interpretation*, 2nd ed. (Indianapolis: Bobbs-Merrill, 1980).

Walther, C.F.W. *Law and Gospel,* Herbert J. A. Bouman, tr. (St. Louis: Concordia Publishing House, 1981).

Ward, Richard F. "A New Look at an Ancient Practice: Public Reading in a Plugged in Church," *Doxology* 18 (2001): 30-48.

Williams, Tyler F. *A Form-Critical Classification of the Psalms According to Hermann Gunkel* (November 2006), accessed 18 April 2011, http://biblical-studies.ca/pdfs/Gunkel_Classification_of_the_Psalms.pdf.

Winger, Thomas. "The Spoken Word: What's Up with Orality?" *Concordia Journal* (April 2003): 133-151.

Endnotes

1   All scripture quotations, unless otherwise indicated, are taken from the New King James Version®. Copyright © 1982 by Thomas Nelson, Inc. Used by permission. All rights reserved.

2   Gayle Felton, "Which Translation is Best?" *The Upper Room* (August 2007). doi:http://www.upperroom.org/reflections/default.asp?act=display_content&itemid=180268.

3   Charlotte I. Lee, *Oral Reading of the Scriptures* (New York: Houghton, Mifflin, Harcourt, 1974).

4   Curry, Samuel Silas. *Vocal and Literary Interpretation of the Bible* (New York: MacMillan, 1903).

5   Dietrich Bonhoeffer, *Life Together* (New York: Harper & Row, 1954), 67.

6   Christopher K. Lensch, "The Public Reading of Scripture," *WRS Journal* 7/1 (Feb 2000): 19-22. URL: http://wrs.edu/resources/wrs-journal/.

7   Clayton J. Schmit, *Public Reading of Scripture: A Handbook* (Nashville, Tennessee: Abingdon Press, 2002), 39.

8   Richard F. Ward, "A New Look at an Ancient Practice: Public Reading in a Plugged in Church," *Doxology 18* (2001): 34. URL: http://www.saint-luke.org/documents/ward.pdf.

9   Billy Collins, "How to Read a Poem Out Loud" *The Library of Congress, Poetry 180 (Feb 2004)*: accessed 17 April 2012, http://www.loc.gov/poetry/180/p180-howtoread.html

10 You can test this by doing a simple word count. Choose any six verse passage in Scripture, and count the verbs, nouns (including pronouns), adjectives, and adverbs. How many do you find? Most likely, you will find that nouns and verbs outnumber adjectives and adverbs by a seven to one ratio.

11 William J. Bausch, *In the Beginning, There Were Stories: Thoughts about the Oral Tradition of the Bible* (Mystic, Connecticut: Twenty-Third Publications, 2004), 57-60.

12 Charlotte I. Lee, *Oral Reading of the Scriptures* (New York: Houghton Mifflin, 1974), 1.

13 Leland Ryken, *How to Read the Bible as Literature . . . and Get More Out of It* (Grand Rapids, Michigan: Zondervan, 1984), 34-35.

14 Barry McWilliams, "Discerning the Story Structures in the Narrative Literature of the Bible," *The Art of Telling Stories,*" 2002. Accessed 25 March 2011, http://www.eldrbarry.net/.

15 Gordon Fee and Douglas Stuart, *How to Read the Bible for All its Worth,* 2nd Ed (Grand Rapids, Michigan: Zondervan, 1993), 74.

16 Ryken, 145.

17 Schmit, Clayton, *Public Reading of Scripture: A Handbook* (Nashville: Abingdon Press, 2002).

18 Charlotte I. Lee, *Oral Reading of the Scriptures* (Boston: Houghton Mifflin, 1974), 89.

19 McWilliams.

20 Lee, 95.

21 Lee, 96.

22 Ryken, 91.

23 Lee, 143.

24 S. S. Curry, *Vocal and Literary Interpretation of the Bible* (New York: MacMillan, 1903), 86.

25 Morris A. Inch, *The Literature and Meaning of Scripture,* Morris A. Inch and C. Hassell Bullock, ed. (Grand Rapids, Michigan: Baker Book House, 1981), 84.

26 Curry, 87.

27 Curry, 86.

28 Ryken, 90.

29 Lowth, Robert. *Lectures on the Sacred Poetry of the Hebrews.* Trans. G. Gregory, 1839, in *Landmarks of World Literature: The Bible* by Stephen Prickett and Robert Barnes (Cambridge, England: Cambridge University Press, 1991), 94.

30 Curry, 67.

31 Grenville J. R. Kent, Paul J. Kissling, and Laurence A. Turner, *Reclaiming the Old Testament for Christian Preaching* (Downers Grove, Illinois: IVP Academic, 2010), 102.

32 Curry, 69.

33 Gordon D. Fee and Douglas K. Stuart, *How to Read the Bible for All Its Worth: A Guide to Understanding the Bible* (Grand Rapids, Michigan: Zondervan, 1982), 149.

34 Ryken, 165.

35 Ryken, 166.

36 George Ricker Berry, "The Apocalyptic Literature of the Old Testament," *Journal of Biblical Literature* 62 , no. 1 (January 1, 1943): 9.

37 Berry, 9.

38 Curry, 72.

39 Walter Robert Roehrs and Martin H. Franzmann, *Concordia Self-Study Commentary* (St. Louis: Concordia Publishing House), 442.

[40] Roehrs and Franzmann, 442.

[41] D. Guthrie and J.A. Motyer, eds., *The New Bible Commentary: Revised* (Grand Rapids, Michigan: Wm. B. Eerdmans Publishing, 1970), 773.

[42] Roehrs and Franzmann, 640.

[43] Robert H. Gundry, *A Survey of the New Testament* (Grand Rapids, Michigan: Zondervan, 1970), 113.

[44] Gilbert G. Bilezikian, "Interpreting Apocalyptic Literature," in *The Literature and Meaning of Scripture* , ed. Morris A. Inch and C. Hassell Bullock (Grand Rapids, Michigan: Baker Book House, 1981), 268.

[45] Berry, 16.

[46] Roehrs and Franzmann, 442.

[47] Curry, 76.